Wholey

FACE MASKS

Holistic Skincare for Wellness and Beauty

WITH 50 EASY DIY FACE MASK RECIPES

LADONNA NATURALE

WHOLEY FACE MASKS:

Holistic Skincare for Wellness and Beauty

LaDonna Naturale

First published by Otis Publishing 2024

Copyright © 2024 by LaDonna Naturale

First edition

This book was professionally typeset on Reedsy.
Find out more at reedsy.com

Contents

Introduction

Every year, millions of us apply creams, serums, and masks to our skin, unknowingly exposing ourselves to a cocktail of chemicals that could have long-term health effects. Did you know that a typical beauty product can contain over 30 chemicals, many of which have been linked to skin irritation, hormonal imbalances, and even more serious health concerns? This startling fact was the catalyst for my journey into the realm of holistic skincare, a journey I now invite you to join with the creation of "Wholey Face Masks."

"Wholey Face Masks" is more than just a catchy name; it's a philosophy. It symbolizes a return to nature, emphasizing the use of whole, pure, and non-toxic ingredients to nourish our skin. In a sea of skincare products that promise beauty at the expense of our health, "Wholey Face Masks" stands out by offering a path to wellness and beauty, intertwined and inseparable.

My motivation for writing this book stems from a deep-rooted desire to share the knowledge I've gained about the hidden dangers lurking in our skincare routines. I've seen firsthand the transformative power of switching to natural, homemade face masks, and I'm passionate about empowering you with this knowledge. By including 50 to 100 simple, natural, and effective face mask recipes, my goal is to equip you with the tools to take control of your skincare, turning your home into a sanctuary of wellness and beauty.

This book is dedicated to you—adults, teens, and women who have ever felt overwhelmed by the endless array of chemical-laden beauty products. Your concerns, struggles, and successes have inspired me. Your desire for a healthier, more sustainable approach to beauty has shaped the content of this book, making it a collective journey toward holistic skincare.

Structured to guide you through the murky waters of cosmetic ingredients and their effects on health, this book lays a solid foundation before diving into the heart of natural skincare practices. You'll find detailed discussions on harmful chemicals and a treasure trove of face mask recipes catering to different skin types and concerns. Each recipe is designed with simplicity in mind, using ingredients that are easily accessible and steps that anyone can follow. Moreover, you'll learn how to customize these masks to suit your unique skin care needs perfectly.

By the end of this book, you'll have a deeper understanding of the impact of chemicals on your skin and health and possess a powerful toolkit for crafting your own natural skincare solutions. This isn't just about making face masks; it's about embracing a lifestyle prioritizing wellness, sustainability, and self-care.

As we embark on this journey together, I'm reminded of my transition from commercial beauty products to the enriching world of natural skincare. It was a journey filled with discoveries, challenges, and profound satisfaction. I hope that by sharing these insights and recipes, I can inspire you to take the first step towards a more holistic approach to beauty —one that celebrates the power of nature and the resilience of our skin.

Together, let's redefine beauty, making it not just skin deep but a reflection of our overall wellness and vitality. Welcome to "Wholey Face Masks."

Chapter 1: Unveiling the Truth About Commercial Skincare Products

As you stand in front of your vanity mirror, applying your favorite moisturizer or serum, you might be unaware of the silent dialogue between your skin and your products. This chapter peels back the glossy exterior of the skincare industry to reveal a less talked-about reality: the prevalence of harmful chemicals in many commercial skincare products. These substances, found in everyday items, are not inert; they interact with our bodies in ways we are only beginning to understand. Here, we will explore the chemical constituents of your skincare regimen, question the laissez-faire attitude of regulatory bodies, and empower you to make informed choices about the products you trust on your skin.

The Chemical Culprits: Naming and Shaming Toxins in Your Vanity

Identification of Harmful Chemicals

In the quest for eternal youth and flawless skin, many of us turn to products that promise miraculous results. However, these potions can be double-edged swords. Commonly used chemicals in skincare products include parabens, sulfates, and phthalates. Parabens, used as preservatives in cosmetics, mimic estrogen and can disrupt hormonal balance, potentially leading to reproductive issues and increased cancer risk. Sulfates, which create the lather and foam in cleansers and shampoos, strip the skin and hair of natural oils, leading to dryness and irritation. Phthalates, often hidden under the term "fragrance," are plasticizers that disrupt the endocrine system, affecting development and fertility. These chemicals are commonplace in countless beauty products, from face washes to moisturizers and makeup.

The Role of These Chemicals in Products

Why are such harmful chemicals so widely used in beauty products? The answer lies in their functional benefits to the product and cost-effectiveness for manufacturers. Parabens extend shelf life, preventing the growth of bacteria and fungi, which is essential for the long-term storage of products. Sulfates are effective cleansing agents that remove dirt and oil, offering the satisfying foaming action consumers associate with cleanliness. Phthalates help fragrances last longer, enhancing the sensoryappeal of products. These benefits make them attractive to cosmetic manufacturers focused on the bottom line rather than long-term health implications.

Regulatory Oversight and Gaps

The regulatory landscape for cosmetic products is surprisingly lenient in many parts of the world, including the United States, where the Food and Drug Administration (FDA) does not require pre-market testing or approval of cosmetics. This means that the safety of the ingredients is often determined by the manufacturers themselves, leading to potential conflicts of interest and a lack of accountability. The European Union has taken a more proactive stance by banning over 1,300 chemicals in cosmetics known or suspected to cause cancer, genetic mutation, reproductive harm, or congenital disabilities, unlike the FDA, which has only banned or restricted 11. This disparity highlights significant gaps in the regulatory frameworks that govern what is safe for consumers.

Consumer Awareness and Action

In the face of these regulatory gaps, the bulk of responsibility often falls on you, the consumer, to become more vigilant about the products you use. Becoming label-savvy—learning to identify harmful chemicals in ingredient lists—is crucial in protecting your health. However, reading labels is not always straightforward, as many chemicals can be hidden under generic terms like "fragrance." Advocating for more transparent labeling and safer products is therefore essential. By choosing products from companies that disclose their ingredients transparently and supporting legislative changes requiring stricter regulations, you contribute to a more significant movement towards safer beauty products. Your choices have power, influencing market trends and encouraging companies to prioritize consumer health over harmful chemicals.

As you transition from merely a consumer to an informed advocate, remember that the products you apply to your skin are more than just superficial treatments; they are substances that interact with your body's largest organ. By choosing wisely and advocating for change, you can protect your skin and overall health, setting a new standard in the beauty industry that values well-being as the most accurate form of beauty.

Skin Deep: How Topical Toxins Affect Our Body

The comforting routine of daily skincare, a ritual many embrace, often overlooks a critical aspect of our biology: our skin is not just a protective barrier but a permeable membrane that can absorb substances directly into the bloodstream. When we apply lotions, serums, and creams, their ingredients don't merely sit on the surface. Instead, they penetrate the skin, entering the circulatory system, where they can exert systemic effects on the body. This absorption process highlights a significant concern regarding the harmful chemicals in skincare products. Once absorbed, substances like parabens and phthalates do not remain confined to the dermal layers; they travel through our bodies, potentially disrupting normal biological functions.

This systemic absorption can have profound implications over time. Research increasingly points to the long-term health effects of continuous exposure to these chemical agents. For instance, studies have linked certain chemicals in skincare products to hormonal imbalances. These disruptions can manifest as altered puberty timing, fertility issues, and even increased risks of hormone-related cancers such as breast and ovarian cancer. Moreover, some chemicals are suspected carcinogens or have been linked to developmental and reproductive toxicity. The cumulative effect of daily, long-term exposure can be significant, raising concerns about the safety of these substances, especially when safer alternatives may not be readily available or promoted.

The risk extends with particular severity to vulnerable populations such as pregnant women, infants, and individuals with pre-existing health conditions. During pregnancy, for example, the chemicals absorbed through the skin can cross the placental barrier, affecting fetal development and being passed on to the infant through breastfeeding. Infants and children are susceptible to chemical exposures because their bodies and organ systems are still developing, which can make them more susceptible to developmental and health issues later in life. Individuals with pre-existing conditions such as eczema or hormonal imbalances might experience exacerbated symptoms or further imbalances due to certain chemicals in skincare products' disruptive nature.

Given these considerable concerns, the advocacy for natural and non-toxic skincare products becomes not just a matter of personal preference but a pressing health imperative.

Natural skincare products, ideally, contain safe ingredients to absorb into the skin and can also offer therapeutic benefits. Ingredients like coconut oil, aloe vera, and shea butter provide moisturization and have healing properties without the adverse effects associated with many synthetic chemicals. Furthermore, the move towards natural skin care products supports not only individual health but also the health of our environment by reducing the chemical load on our water systems and soil, thus promoting a healthier ecosystem.

Transitioning to natural skincare products involves understanding the potential risks associated with synthetic chemicals and recognizing the benefits of natural ingredients. It calls for a shift in perception—from viewing skincare as merely cosmetic to seeing it as an integral part of overall health maintenance. This shift is crucial today as we navigate through various products, each promising beauty, yet not all guaranteeing safety. As consumers, gaining knowledge about the ingredients in our skincare and making informed decisions is an empowering step towards enhancing our beauty and safeguarding our health and our families.

The Allergic Reaction Epidemic: Connecting Skin Health to Product Ingredients

In recent years, there has been a noticeable increase in the prevalence of skin allergies and sensitivities. This trend is profoundly concerning to those affected, healthcare providers, and researchers. Statistics indicate that nearly 20% of the population in industrialized nations is affected by allergic contact dermatitis, and the numbers are rising. This surge is often linked to the complex mix of chemicals present in everyday skincare products. Many of these substances, while creating appealing textures and scents, can also trigger adverse reactions, disrupting our lives with uncomfortable and sometimes severe skin issues.

Certain elements stand out as repeat offenders among the myriad of ingredients in skincare products. Fragrances, for instance, are a significant cause of allergic reactions. Despite their ability to make a product more attractive to the senses, they can provoke symptoms ranging from mild irritation to severe dermatitis. Similarly, preservatives such as methylisothiazolino ne (MI) are known to cause issues. These chemicals are essential for prolonging shelf life but can be aggressive on sensitive skin, leading to redness, itching, and other allergic responses. The list includes formaldehyde releasers, which, while less commonly used today, still appear in specific formulations and are notorious for their sensitizing potential.

The personal implications of these reactions are profound. Consider the story of a middle-aged woman who, after years of using a seemingly benign night cream, developed a rash that persisted for months before it was traced back to a newly added fragrance in the formula. Or a young man whose excitement over a popular branded moisturizer turned into a painful ordeal with contact dermatitis due to a common preservative. These stories echo in dermatologists' offices worldwide, highlighting a growing disconnect between the allure of modern skincare products and their potential health risks.

To combat this issue, it's crucial to adopt preventive measures and become proactive about the ingredients in skincare products. Start by reading labels meticulously. Ingredients like 'fragrance' or 'parfum' on a label can be a red flag, as these terms can mask numerous chemicals that companies aren't required to disclose individually. Opting for products labeled as 'fragrance-free' or 'for sensitive skin' can sometimes minimize risks, but it's not foolproof—a thorough ingredient check is still advisable. They also conduct a patch test before a new product can prevent potential reactions. Apply a small amount of the product on a discreet area of skin, such as the inner wrist or behind the ear, and wait 48 hours to observe any adverse reactions.

This growing awareness and the increasing incidence of allergic reactions have steered many consumers toward more natural alternatives. Ingredients derived from nature tend to be gentler on the skin since they are less likely to contain aggressive chemicals. However, it's important to note that 'natural' doesn't always mean non-allergenic. Essential oils, for example, are natural but can be potent allergens. Therefore, understanding synthetic and natural ingredients' properties and potential impacts is vital to choosing safer skincare products.

Navigating the complex world of skincare ingredients is more than a matter of personal beauty—it's a significant aspect of health care. As we continue to see the rise in allergic reactions and sensitivities, the dialogue between consumers and manufacturers must evolve. The demand for transparency in labeling and the push for formulations that respect skin health are becoming louder, driven by the voices of those affected and supported by the insights of dermatological research. In this way, the narrative of skincare is slowly shifting towards a focus on safety and sensitivity, paving the way for products that honor the skin's health as much as their aesthetic appeal.

Breaking Free: The Shift Towards Natural Skincare Solutions

The allure of natural skincare has captured the imagination and attention of consumers worldwide, a trend fueled by growing concerns over the health implications of synthetic chemicals in beauty products. As awareness of these risks increases, so does the demand for skin care products formulated from natural and organic ingredients. This shift is not merely a fashion or marketing trend but a substantive move towards healthier, more sustainable beauty practices. People are becoming more conscientious about what they eat and what they apply to their skin, seeking products that align with a more holistic approach to health.

The benefits of turning to natural skincare are manifold. On a personal health level, natural skin care products typically contain fewer irritants and toxic chemicals, making them gentler on the skin. They often come packed with beneficial nutrients, like antioxidants and vitamins derived from natural sources such as fruits, oils, and herbs. These ingredients can help nourish and repair the skin, promoting a healthier complexion without exposing the body to harmful synthetic chemicals. Moreover, natural skincare products are frequently more environmentally sustainable. They tend to be produced using organically farmed ingredients that do not employ pesticides or herbicides, practices that can contaminate water, air, and soil and disrupt local ecosystems. The production methods often prioritize ethical practices, including cruelty-free testing and fair labor conditions, making them a more morally conscientious choice.

However, transitioning to a natural skincare regimen can pose challenges. One of the most significant barriers may be the cost. Natural and organic ingredients are often more expensive to produce and source, leading to higher retail prices for the end products. This can be a deterrent for those accustomed to the relatively lower prices of conventional skincare products. Another challenge is finding natural skincare products as effective as their chemical-laden counterparts. The market is flooded with products claiming to be 'natural' or 'organic,' but not all deliver on these promises or provide the desired skincare results. This discrepancy can lead to frustration and skepticism about the efficacy of natural skincare products.

Despite these challenges, transitioning to a natural skincare routine can be rewarding and health-promoting. To start, learning how to read and interpret product labels is crucial. The terms 'natural' and 'organic' are not regulated universally, meaning manufacturers can use them loosely. Look for products certified by reputable organizations, and familiarize yourself with the names of common natural ingredients so you can identify them on labels. Begin by incorporating one or two natural products into your routine to see how your skin responds before completely overhauling your skincare regimen. This gradual approach helps to mitigate the cost of transition and allows you to test the effectiveness of different products.

Moreover, many effective natural skincare solutions can be made at home using simple ingredients from your kitchen or garden. This DIY approach gives you complete control over what goes on your skin and provides a fun and empowering way to take charge of your beauty regimen. The possibilities are endless, from homemade face masks made with avocados and honey to scrubs crafted from coffee grounds and coconut oil. They can be tailored to suit your specific skin needs and preferences.

As you explore the world of natural skincare, remember that every small change contributes to more considerable wellness and environmental benefits. By choosing natural skincare, you are fostering your health and beauty and supporting sustainable practices that respect the planet and its inhabitants. This mindful approach to beauty is more than skin deep—it's a testament to your daily values. As this movement grows, it continues to reshape the landscape of the skincare industry, steering it towards greater transparency, accountability, and respect for human and environmental health. Embracing natural skincare is thus not just a personal choice but a collective step towards a more sustainable and ethically conscious world.

Chapter 2: The Philosophy of Holistic Beauty

Imagine stepping into a world where beauty transcends the superficial layers of makeup and skincare to embrace the essence of your overall well-being. In this chapter, we explore the concept of holistic beauty, a philosophy that integrates the health of your body, mind, and environment into your beauty regimen. Unlike conventional beauty standards that often focus solely on external appearance, holistic beauty invites you to consider a broader spectrum of health and wellness as integral components of looking and feeling beautiful.

Beyond the Surface: Holistic Beauty as a Lifestyle Choice

Defining Holistic Beauty

Holistic beauty is an approach that seeks to harmonize physical appearance with inner well-being and environmental health.

This philosophy recognizes that true beauty reflects the body's overall health and the choices we make daily. It extends beyond the cosmetics and procedures that adorn the outer self and delves into nurturing the body from within and respecting the world around us. By embracing holistic beauty, you engage in practices that enhance your natural appearance while promoting long-term health and sustainability.

The Role of Lifestyle Factors

The journey to holistic beauty is paved with your choices about how you live your life. Diet, exercise, and stress management are pivotal in shaping your health and, by extension, your appearance. A balanced diet rich in antioxidants and anti-inflammatory foods can combat aging and give your skin a natural glow. Regular physical activity increases blood flow, helping to nourish skin cells and keep them vital. Exercise also helps reduce stress, exacerbating skin problems like acne and eczema. By integrating these elements into your daily routine, you enhance your physical appearance and improve your mental and emotional well-being, all of which are visible in your skin, your body's largest organ.

Environmental and Ethical Considerations

As you adopt a holistic approach to beauty, it becomes crucial to consider the impact of your beauty routine on the environment. The beauty industry is notorious for excessive waste, harmful chemicals, and unethical practices, all of which can contradict the principles of holistic beauty. By choosing sustainably sourced products made with natural ingredients and packaged in eco-friendly materials, you contribute to a healthier planet. Ethical considerations also extend to the labor practices behind your beauty products. Supporting companies that ensure fair wages and safe working conditions reflects a commitment to global well-being, aligning your beauty routine with your values.

Steps to Adopt a Holistic Beauty Lifestyle

Transitioning to a holistic beauty lifestyle requires mindfulness and a willingness to embrace new practices that support your health and the environment. Begin by assessing your current beauty regimen and identifying areas where you can make more health-conscious choices. Switch to skincare products free of harmful chemicals and prioritize organic and natural ingredients. Incorporate the practice of reading labels and researching the ethical practices of the companies you support into your routine.

Engaging in routine self-care practices can significantly enhance your holistic beauty journey. Allocate time each day for activities that nourish your body and soul, whether practicing yoga, meditating, or simply taking a moment to breathe deeply and center yourself. These practices help reduce stress and promote a balanced, calm state of mind reflected in your outer beauty.

Moreover, consider the impact of your diet on your skin and overall health. Integrating foods rich in vitamins, minerals, and antioxidants can dramatically improve your skin's health. Drink plenty of water to stay hydrated, and consider reducing your intake of processed foods and sugars, which can inflame your skin and accelerate aging.

Finally, holistic beauty is about continuous learning and adapting. Stay informed about new research and trends in natural and ethical beauty care. Engage with communities that share your values, and be open to trying new products and practices that align with your holistic goals. Remember, each small step contributes to a more excellent balance between your beauty routine and overall well-being, creating a more beautiful you inside and out.

Visualizing Your Holistic Beauty Path

Consider creating a vision board to help you visualize and plan your holistic beauty transformation. Gather images, quotes, and items representing your beauty goals and the lifestyle you aspire to. This board can remind you daily of your commitment to holistic beauty and inspire you to maintain your practices. It's a simple yet powerful tool that keeps you connected to your objectives and motivates you to continue on your path to holistic wellness.

The Mind-Skin Connection: How Stress Affects Your Glow

When you experience stress, your mood is not the only thing that suffers—your skin often shows signs, too. The connection between stress and skin health is significant and scientifically recognized. It involves a complex interplay of hormones and inflammatory responses that can dramatically impact the appearance and health of your skin. When stressed, your body produces higher levels of cortisol, known as the stress hormone. This hormone can increase oil production in your skin glands, exacerbating conditions like acne.

Moreover, cortisol and other stress-related hormones can degrade collagen and elastin, two critical proteins that maintain skin elasticity and firmness. This degradation can accelerate aging, leading to premature wrinkles and sagging skin. Additionally, stress can trigger or worsen inflammatory skin conditions such as eczema and psoriasis by prompting the body to release substances that inflame the skin and disrupt its natural balance.

The real-life implications of these physiological processes are evident in everyday scenarios. Consider someone with a high-pressure job who experiences chronic stress. Over time, they may notice their skin becoming oilier, leading to breakouts, or they may see an increase in flare-ups of eczema or rosacea. For many, these skin issues are not just a cosmetic concern but also a significant source of additional stress, creating a frustrating cycle where stress exacerbates skin problems, and skin problems, in turn, increase stress levels. This cycle can be particularly challenging for teenagers and young adults, who may already be sensitive to changes in their appearance and how peers perceive them.

Incorporating regular stress management techniques into your daily routine can be incredibly beneficial to combat the effects of stress on the skin. Meditation, for example, is a powerful tool for calming the mind and reducing stress. It involves focusing your attention and eliminating the stream of jumbled thoughts that may be crowding your mind and causing stress. Meditation can help you achieve a state of calm, peace, and balance that benefits your emotional well-being and overall health—and, by extension, your skin. Yoga, another effective stress management technique, combines physical poses, controlled breathing, and meditation or relaxation. It might help reduce stress and lower blood pressure and heart rate. Like meditation, yoga is known for promoting relaxation and reducing stress levels, which can lead to more transparent, more radiant skin.

Regular exercise is another crucial element in managing stress and promoting skin health. Physical activity helps increase blood flow, which nourishes skin cells and keeps them vital. Blood flow also helps remove waste products, including free radicals, from working cells. This can help decrease the likeli- hood of stress-related skin issues and promote a more youthful, vibrant complexion. Exercise doesn't have to be intense to be effective; even a daily walk or short bike ride can yield noticeable benefits.

Personal success stories abound from individuals who have integrated these stress-reduction techniques into their lives and seen remarkable improvements in their skin. One notable example is a woman in her late twenties who suffered from persistent acne due to her high-stress job in a legal firm. After incorporating a routine of yoga and short meditation sessions into her daily schedule, she noticed a significant reduction in her stress levels and a clear improvement in her skin. Her acne began to clear up, and her overall skin tone improved, reflecting the inner peace and balance she had achieved through her dedication to managing stress.

These stories underscore the powerful impact that stress management can have on skin health. By understanding and mitigating the effects of stress through practical, everyday actions, you can help maintain your skin's beauty and vitality. This approach enhances your physical appearance and contributes to a healthier, more balanced lifestyle.

Beauty from Within: Nutrition and Skin Health

Our diet plays an indisputably crucial role when considering the factors contributing to skin health. What you choose to nourish your body daily doesn't just influence your energy levels and overall health; it also significantly impacts the quality and appearance of your skin. To truly embrace a holistic approach to beauty, understanding the nutrients essential for maintaining and enhancing skin health is vital, as is recognizing which foods can detract from our skin's natural vitality.

Nutrients Essential for Skin Health

A well-rounded diet rich in specific vitamins and omega-3 fatty acids is foundational for radiant, healthy skin. Vitamins A, C, and E are renowned for their skin-enhancing properties. Vitamin A, found abundantly in carrots, sweet potatoes, and leafy greens, is crucial in skin repair and maintenance. It helps prevent sun damage by interrupting the process that breaks down collagen. Since the body converts beta-carotene (found in plants) into vitamin A, incorporating a variety of colorful vegetables into your meals can boost your vitamin A levels, contributing to protected and vibrant skin.

Vitamin C is another powerhouse for skin health, known for its potent antioxidant properties and role in collagen synthesis. Brightly colored fruits, such as oranges, strawberries, kiwis, and vegetables, like bell peppers and broccoli, are excellent sources of vitamin C. Regular consumption can help ward off signs of aging and promote a bright, youthful complexion.

Vitamin E, found in nuts and seeds like almonds and sunflower seeds, complements vitamin C by acting as a major antioxidant that protects the skin from damage caused by free radicals and environmental aggressors like UV rays and pollution. Vitamins C and E can significantly decelerate the skin's aging process, maintaining elasticity and reducing the visibility of lines and wrinkles.

Omega-3 fatty acids are vital for maintaining skin health and have strong anti-inflammatory properties that can help reduce acne and other inflammatory skin conditions. Flaxseeds, chia seeds, and fatty fish like salmon are rich in omega-3s and can be integral to a diet that supports robust, healthy skin.

Dietary Patterns for Optimal Skin Health

Adopting a dietary pattern that promotes skin health doesn't require drastic changes—simple adjustments and more thoughtful food choices can make a significant difference. A diet rich in fruits and vegetables provides the vitamins needed for skin health and antioxidants that protect the skin from harmful radicals that can accelerate aging. Hydration is pivotal in maintaining skin elasticity and vibrance, so drinking plenty of water throughout the day is essential. Additionally, including healthy fats from sources like avocados and olive oil can help keep your skin moisturized and supple.

One practical approach to ensuring a skin-healthy diet is to in- corporate a variety of whole foods. Whole grains, lean proteins, and a rainbow of fruits and vegetables can create a balanced diet that supports skin health. Such diversity supplies a rich spectrum of skin-boosting nutrients and contributes to overall health, reflecting positively on your skin.

Foods to Avoid

Some foods can enhance skin health, but others can detract from it. High-glycemic foods, such as white bread, sugary treats, and other processed carbohydrates, can trigger insulin spikes, which may exacerbate skin inflammation. Similarly, dairy products have been linked to acne in some people, possibly due to hormones present in milk. While the exact relationship between diet and acne can vary significantly among individuals, paying attention to how your skin reacts to certain foods and adjusting your diet accordingly can be beneficial.

Trans fats, often found in fried foods and baked goods, can contribute to inflammation and might make skin conditions worse. Reducing or eliminating these from your diet can help to improve not only your skin health but also your overall cardiovascular health.

Recipes and Meal Ideas

Integrating skin-healthy foods into your diet can be both delicious and uncomplicated. For breakfast, consider a smoothie that combines spinach, a rich source of vitamin A, with strawberries and oranges for a vitamin C boost. Add a tablespoon of flaxseed for omega-3 fatty acids, and you have a powerful, skin-healthy start to your day.

For lunch or dinner, a salad with mixed greens, sliced almonds, and avocado can provide a satisfying mix of vitamins E and C and healthy fats. Top it with salmon or grilled chicken for protein and additional omega-3s. For a snack, opt for carrot sticks with hummus or a handful of sunflower seeds, which are excellent for your skin.

Creating meals that are good for your skin doesn't require unique recipes or unavailable ingredients; it simply involves making mindful choices about incorporating a variety of nutrients into your daily diet. By choosing foods loaded with antioxidants, healthy fats, and vitamins, you can ensure that your diet supports your health and your skin's natural beauty.

The Ritual of Self-Care: Making Time for Your Skin

In the bustling rhythm of modern life, carving out moments for self-care often falls by the wayside, yet it remains an essential pillar of holistic beauty. This concept extends beyond mere skincare; it encompasses a broader commitment to nurturing your body and spirit. Recognizing the vital role of self-care is the first step toward integrating it into your daily routine, ensuring your skin—and overall well-being—reaps the benefits.

Self-care is fundamentally about taking time to attend to your personal needs, a practice that is far from selfish. Instead, it's a crucial aspect of maintaining balance and health. When you regularly engage in self-care, you provide your body, including your skin, the opportunity to rejuvenate and repair. This can be as simple as dedicating time each evening to a skincare regimen that includes cleansing, moisturizing, and treating the skin with nutrient-rich products. However, proper self-care goes deeper, involving activities that relieve stress and enhance your mental and emotional well-being, such as reading, journaling, or engaging in a hobby you love.

Creating a self-care routine that resonates with your lifestyle and personal preferences is critical. Begin by identifying the times of day when you feel most in need of a pause or most likely to benefit from a self-care activity. For many, this might be in the morning, setting a positive tone for the day, or in the evening, helping to unwind before bed. Integrate skincare practices with other soothing activities. For instance, while a face mask does its work, you might listen to calming music, meditate, or sip herbal tea. This enhances the skin's appearance and contributes a more profound sense of relaxation and contentment.

Incorporating mindfulness into your skincare routine transforms it from a mundane task into a rich, stimulating experience. Mindfulness involves being fully present in the moment and aware of your senses and thoughts without judgment. When applying skincare products, focus on the product's texture, the sensation as it touches your skin, and the smell. This practice increases the enjoyment of the routine and can make you more attuned to your skin's needs and responses to different products. Over time, this heightened awareness can lead to better choices for your skin type and concerns.

Balancing self-care with a hectic schedule might seem daunting, but it's achievable with some strategic planning. Identify small pockets of time in your day dedicated to self-care. Even five to ten minutes can be enough for a few deep breaths and some facial stretches, which can refresh your mind and skin. Consider multitasking in a way that allows you to relax and benefit from the activity. For example, wearing a hydrating sheet mask while preparing breakfast or listening to an audiobook can efficiently use time without feeling rushed. Remember, the goal is to make self-care a non-negotiable part of your day, akin to eating or sleeping.

By embedding these practices into your routine, you enhance your skin's health and improve your quality of life. The self-care ritual offers a daily opportunity to retreat from the pressures of life, reconnect with yourself, and nurture your physical appearance and inner well-being. As you continue to explore and expand your self-care practices, you'll likely discover that these moments of pause and care are beneficial and essential for maintaining balance in your busy life.

As this chapter closes, reflect on how integrating self-care into your daily life is not just about enhancing your outward appearance but is deeply connected to nurturing your overall well-being. These practices help forge a stronger connection with yourself, making you better equipped to handle the stresses of daily life. With this foundation, you're ready to explore further into holistic beauty, continuing to build on the principles of wellness, mindfulness, and environmental consciousness. The next chapter will guide you through the practical steps of implementing these holistic practices into your beauty routine, ensuring they become a seamless part of your journey toward wellness and beauty, enhancing how you look and feel.

Chapter 3: The Natural Pantry

Imagine your kitchen not just as a place for culinary creation but as a sanctuary where beauty begins. This chapter explores how everyday superfoods, those heroes hidden in plain sight on your pantry shelves or nestled in your refrigerator, are powerful allies in your skincare regimen. These natural treasures, packed with vitamins, antioxidants, and essential fats, are the cornerstone of nurturing your skin from the outside in. Let's delve into how integrating these nutrient-rich foods into your skincare routine can transform your skin's health, making it as radiant as it is resilient.

Superfoods for Super Skin: Avocado, Honey, and Beyond

Nutrient-rich Avocados

Avocados, a staple in healthy diets, are just as beneficial for our skin as they are for our overall health. Known for their rich content of healthy fats, particularly monounsaturated fats, avocados offer profound benefits in maintaining skin elasticity and combating dryness. These fats are essential building blocks for skin cells, forming a barrier that keeps moisture and harmful elements out, ensuring your skin remains hydrated and plump. But the benefits don't end there; avocados are also packed with vitamins E and C, both known for protecting skin from oxidative damage due to exposure to UV rays and environmental pollution. The high antioxidant content of vitamin E and the collagen-stimulating properties of vitamin C make avocados a powerhouse in supporting skin health and vitality. Applying avocado-based masks can nourish the skin deeply, leaving it supple and vibrant. For a simple home remedy, mash a ripe avocado and use it on your face as a moisturizing mask, or mix it with other ingredients like honey or yogurt for added benefits.

The Healing Properties of Honey

Honey, nature's sweetener, is your skin's friend thanks to its antibacterial and moisturizing properties. This golden elixir supports skin health by acting as a natural humectant, drawing moisture into the skin and retaining it there, which helps to ward off dryness and keep the skin soft and dewy. Moreover, honey is rich in antioxidants and bioactive compounds that provide it with mild antibacterial properties, making it an excellent ingredient for acne treatment and prevention. It can help manage skin conditions like acne by preventing bacterial infections and calming inflammation. A honey face mask, simple yet effective, can be made by spreading a thin layer of raw honey on clean skin. Leave it on for 10-15 minutes, then rinse with warm water for nourished, glowing skin.

Superfoods Variety

Beyond avocados and honey, the realm of superfoods bene-ficial for skin health is vast. Almonds, for instance, are a great source of vitamin E, which helps protect the skin from damaging UV rays and keeps skin cells healthy. They can be ground into a fine powder and mixed with honey or yogurt to create a rejuvenating facial scrub. With its potent anti-inflammatory properties, turmeric is an excellent addition to face masks for reducing redness and calming skin conditions like psoriasis and eczema. Its active compound, curcumin, has strong antioxidant properties, helping to brighten the skin and even out skin tone. Mixing turmeric with a bit of honey and milk can create a paste that leaves the skin radiant and smooth when applied to the face.

Incorporating Superfoods into Skincare

Incorporating these superfoods into your skincare routine doesn't have to be complicated. Many of these ingredients can be combined to enhance their effects. For example, creating a face mask that includes mashed avocado, a teaspoon of honey, and a sprinkle of turmeric can provide moisturizing, antibacterial, and anti-inflammatory benefits. These ingredients are not only practical but also accessible, making it easy to whip up a skincare product in the comfort of your own home. By taking these pantry staples and integrating them into your skincare practices, you harness the natural power of these foods to enhance your skin's health naturally and sustainably.

The Herb Garden: Lavender, Rosemary, and Their Potent Powers

In the serene ambiance of your garden or windowsill, the gentle presence of herbs like lavender and rosemary embellishes the space and brings a bounty of skincare benefits. Lavender, renowned for its dreamy scent and beautiful purple hue, holds calming properties that are a boon for the mind and the skin. Particularly beneficial in your evening skincare routine, lavender can help soothe skin irritations ranging from sunburns to minor cuts and bites. Its natural anti-inflammatory and antiseptic properties make it an excellent choice for calming acne flare-ups, while its calming aroma helps reduce stress and promote a peaceful night's sleep. Incorporating lavender into your skincare routine can be as simple as adding a few drops of essential oil to your nighttime moisturizer or preparing a lavender-infused toner to help soothe and hydrate the skin before bed.

Transitioning to another remarkable herb, rosemary, this culinary favorite is much more than just a flavor enhancer. Known for its refreshing fragrance, rosemary is rich in antioxidants, which help protect skin cells from damage and premature aging caused by environmental stressors like UV rays and pollution. One of the most compelling benefits of rosemary is its ability to stimulate blood circulation. Improved circulation revitalizes the skin, making it appear more vibrant and toned and ensuring that essential nutrients are efficiently distributed throughout the skin cells. For an invigorating morning routine, consider using a facial scrub made from ground rosemary leaves or a few drops of rosemary oil mixed with a carrier oil, which can help rejuvenate the skin and prepare you for the day ahead.

The herb garden offers much more than just lavender and rosemary. Chamomile, with its mild and soothing properties, is perfect for sensitive or irritated skin. It can help reduce redness and calm conditions such as eczema and rosacea. Mint, another versatile herb, is known for its cooling properties, making it ideal for treating inflamed or itchy skin. Additionally, mint's high salicylic acid content makes it effective in preventing and treating acne. These herbs can be used in various forms, from fresh leaves added to homemade masks and toners to dried herbs infused in oils or brewed into potent teas that can be applied directly to the skin.

Growing your herb garden can transform your approach to skincare, ensuring you have fresh, organic herbs at your fingertips. Starting a small herb garden is simpler than you think. Even if space is limited, many herbs thrive in small pots on windowsills or balconies. Begin with herbs that are beneficial for your skin and easy to grow, such as lavender, rosemary, mint, and chamomile. These herbs generally require similar care: well-draining soil, regular watering, and plenty of sunlight. By nurturing these plants, you cultivate ingredients for your skincare and deepen your connection to the natural world, enhancing your overall well-being. Tending to your garden, whether watering, pruning, or harvesting, can be a form of mindfulness, bringing a sense of calm and presence to your daily routine. Moreover, the satisfaction of using skincare products made with herbs from your garden is unparalleled, adding a personalized and satisfying element to your skincare regimen.

Fruits of Beauty: Citrus, Berries, and Papaya for Radiant Skin

Citrus Fruits' Brightening Properties

Stepping into the vibrant world of citrus fruits, it's easy to see why they are celebrated for their invigorating flavors and skin- enhancing benefits. Citrus fruits like lemons and oranges are abundant in vitamin C, a vital nutrient that plays a crucial role in maintaining and restoring radiance to the skin. Vitamin C is pivotal in producing collagen, a protein that gives skin elasticity and firmness. Collagen production naturally decreases as we age, leading to signs of aging such as wrinkles and sagging skin.

Incorporating citrus fruits into your skincare regime provides your skin with the essential vitamin C needed to stimulate collagen production, helping maintain a youthful and vibrant complexion.

Moreover, the natural acids present in citrus fruits make them excellent for brightening and evening out skin tone. These acids gently exfoliate the top layer of dead skin cells, revealing the fresher, brighter skin underneath. This natural exfoliation process can help reduce the appearance of dark spots and hyperpigmentation, giving the skin a more even complexion. To harness these benefits, a simple DIY face mask can be made by combining fresh orange juice with honey and a bit of turmeric. Apply this mixture to the face, leave it on for about 15 minutes, and then wash off with lukewarm water. This brightens the skin and adds a dose of hydration and anti-inflammatory benefits, making it a multifaceted treatment that's easy to whip up at home.

Berries' Antioxidant Power

Turning our attention to berries, these tiny fruits are giants in skincare. Blueberries, raspberries, and strawberries pack powerful antioxidants, crucial in protecting the skin from oxidative stress caused by environmental pollutants and UV radiation. These antioxidants, including vitamins C and E, flavonoids, and phenolic acids, help neutralize harmful free radicals that can lead to premature skin aging. Regularly incorporating berries into your skincare routine can help maintain the skin's integrity, keeping it resilient against environmental stressors that cause fine lines, wrinkles, and dullness.

Berries are beneficial when eaten and can be applied topically in various skincare formulations to enhance their direct benefits to the skin. For an antioxidant-rich face mask, mash a handful of raspberries with a spoon of Greek yogurt and a drizzle of honey. This mixture can be applied to the face for about 20 minutes before rinsing. The yogurt adds a soothing and moisturizing element to the mask, while the honey provides antibacterial properties, making this mask a comprehensive treatment for nourishing and revitalizing the skin.

Papaya's Exfoliating Enzymes

Papaya is another fruit that deserves a spotlight in our natural skincare pantry. Rich in papain, an enzyme with natural exfoliating properties, papaya helps break down inactive proteins and remove dead skin cells. This promotes a smoother, refined skin texture and can help prevent the clogged pores that lead to acne breakouts. Additionally, papaya contains vitamins A, C, and E, which provide further nourishment and antioxidant protection to the skin.

Creating a papaya-based exfoliating mask is simple and effective. Blend a few pieces of ripe papaya into a smooth paste, apply it directly to clean skin, and let it sit for about 15 minutes. Doing a patch test for sensitive skin is advisable first, as the enzymes can be pretty potent. After rinsing the mask off, your skin will feel refreshed and invigorated, with a visible improvement in texture and radiance.

Crafting Fruit-Based Skincare Recipes

When it comes to incorporating fruits into your skincare routine, the possibilities are as vast as your creativity. The key to success is understanding the properties of each fruit and how they can benefit your skin type. Always use fresh, ripe fruits containing the most beneficial nutrients. Handling these ingredients carefully is essential; ensure all fruits are thoroughly washed and adequately prepared to avoid skin irritation.

Storing homemade fruit-based skincare products can be tricky, as they need more preservatives found in commercial products. To ensure safety and efficacy, making small batches of your DIY creations, using them immediately, or storing them in the refrigerator for no more than a couple of days is best. This maintains the potency of the active ingredients and prevents the growth of bacteria. Always use clean utensils and containers when preparing and storing your products to keep them safe and effective.

By exploring the natural benefits of citrus, berries, and papaya, you empower yourself to take control of your skincare routine, using ingredients that are not only effective but also gentle and nourishing. This approach allows you to care for your skin in a way that is in harmony with nature, using the bounty of nutrients provided by these beautiful fruits. Whether you are dealing with dullness, dryness, or signs of aging, the natural pantry offers a variety of solutions that cater to your needs, helping you achieve healthy, glowing skin.

The Oil Well: Exploring the Benefits of Oils in Skincare

Oils have been a cornerstone in beauty rituals across the globe for centuries, prized for their profound effects on skin health and appearance. In this modern age, we revisit these ancient remedies, finding that oils like coconut, almond, and jojoba not only deeply moisturize and nourish but do so without clogging pores, making them perfect even for those with sensitive or acne-prone skin. These carrier oils are the foundation of many skincare products, providing essential hydration that helps maintain the skin's natural barrier. For instance, coconut oil, with its rich content of fatty acids, offers intense hydration and anti-inflammatory properties, making it ideal for soothing dry, itchy, or sensitive skin. Almond oil, light and readily absorbable, is packed with vitamins A and E, which help to repair and protect the skin from oxidative stress and UV damage. Jojoba oil closely mimics the skin's sebum, making it an excellent moisturizer that can help regulate oil production, offering a balanced hydration that is particularly beneficial for oily skin types.

Transitioning into the realm of essential oils, these potent extracts concentrate the healing powers of plants into just a few drops. Tea tree oil, for example, is highly valued for its antibacterial and anti-inflammatory properties, making it an excellent choice for treating acne. By penetrating deeply into the pores, it helps to disinfect and calm the skin, reducing the occurrence and severity of breakouts. Rosehip oil, rich in vitamins C and A, is revered for promoting collagen production and speeding up skin regeneration, making it a potent anti- aging treatment. When incorporating essential oils into your skincare regime, it's crucial to understand the importance of proper dilution. Essential oils are highly concentrated and can irritate if applied directly to the skin. Typically, they should be diluted with a carrier oil, such as jojoba or almond oil, to ensure they are safe and effective.

Choosing the right oil for your skin type is paramount to achieving the best results. Oily skin, for instance, can benefit from lighter oils like jojoba or grapeseed oil, which help regulate oil production without adding excess oil to the skin. On the other hand, dry skin may require more decadent oils like avocado or olive oil, which provide more substantial hydration and help repair the skin's moisture barrier. Sensitive skin needs gentle and non-irritating oils, such as calendula or sunflower oil, known for their soothing properties.

When selecting oils, it's also essential to consider their comedogenic rating, which indicates how likely an oil is to clog pores. Non-comedogenic oils like hemp seed oil can be a safe choice for those prone to acne or with congested skin.

DIY oil blends offer a personalized skincare option that can cater precisely to your needs and preferences. Creating your blend allows you to combine the unique benefits of various oils, tailoring the product to address specific skin concerns. For a simple yet effective hydrating serum, mix jojoba oil with a few drops of rosehip and lavender essential oil; this blend is perfect for improving skin tone and texture while providing a calming, soothing effect. For an acne-fighting oil blend, combine neem oil with tea tree and lavender essential oils; this potent mix can help reduce inflammation and prevent future breakouts.

By exploring the diverse world of carrier and essential oils, You equip yourself with knowledge and tools to enhance your skincare routine. These natural oils offer a versatile, effective, and gentle approach to addressing a wide range of skin concerns, from dryness and aging to acne and sensitivity. By understanding how to select and combine these oils, you can create customized skincare solutions that promote healthier, more radiant skin.

In this chapter, we've traversed the enriching landscape of natural oils, uncovering their myriad benefits for skin health. From the deep moisturizing properties of carrier oils like co-conut and almond to the targeted treatments provided by essential oils such as tea tree and rosehip, we've seen how these natural extracts can transform our skin care practices. The ability to mix and match oils based on skin type and concerns personalizes your skincare regimen. It enhances its effectiveness, ensuring your skin receives precise nourishment.

As we close this chapter, we carry the insights gained into the broader context of holistic skincare. Each natural ingredient we incorporate, and each mindful practice we adopt brings us closer to achieving beauty, wellness, and harmony with nature. In the following chapters, we will continue exploring how various natural elements and practices can be woven into a comprehensive skincare routine that honors our health and the environment. This journey, rich in tradition and modern innovation, promises to reshape our understanding of beauty and its connection to the world around us.

Chapter 4: Sourcing and Sustainability

As you embark on your holistic skincare journey, understanding where your products come from and how they are made is as crucial as knowing their benefits. This chapter delves into eco-conscious skincare shopping, guiding you through the labyrinth of market choices towards more sustainable, ethical practices. Each decision at the checkout can echo a commitment to personal health and planetary well-being. This isn't just shopping; it's a vote for the future of beauty, aligning your skincare routine with the values of environmental stewardship and social responsibility.

The Eco-Conscious Skincare Shopper: A Guide to Buying Sustainably

Identifying Sustainable Brands

Navigating the vast sea of beauty brands claiming sustainability can be overwhelming. Genuinely understanding and identifying which brands are committed to sustainable practices requires a keen eye and informed knowledge. First and foremost, look for transparency in sourcing and production methods. Genuinely sustainable brands are usually open about where they source their ingredients and how they manufacture their products. They often share detailed information about their supply chains and steps to minimize environmental impact.

Another good indicator is the presence of third-party certifications. Certifications such as Ecocert, USDA Organic, or Fair Trade certify that a brand meets specific environmental and ethical standards. For instance, the USDA Organic certification ensures that plant-based products are grown without synthetic pesticides and fertilizers, promoting ecological balance and conserving biodiversity. Familiarizing yourself with these certifications can help you make informed choices about the products you choose to support.

Evaluating Product Labels and Certifications

Understanding product labels is critical to becoming an informed consumer. Labels can tell you a lot about a product's ingredients and the brand's commitment to sustainability. When evaluating labels, look for specific claims like "paraben-free," "sulfate-free," and "phthalate-free." These indicate that the product avoids certain harmful chemicals, which is a good start. However, to truly understand a product's impact, you must consider what is included, not just what's excluded. Ingredients should be easily recognizable or have a clear explanation. For example, ingredients derived from sustainable sources like "organic coconut oil" are preferable to vague terms like "fragrance," which can hide a multitude of synthetic chemicals.

Furthermore, certifications like Fair Trade ensure that products are made concerning people and the planet. Fair Trade certification emphasizes fair wages, safe working conditions, and sustainable community development. Products bearing this label support ethical sourcing and contribute to the welfare of the communities involved in their production.

The Impact of Packaging

The packaging of skincare products plays a significant role in their environmental impact. Opting for recyclable or biodegradable packaging products can significantly reduce your carbon footprint. Many sustainable brands are moving towards using post-consumer recycled materials or innovating with biodegradable options like bamboo and mushroom packaging. When shopping, choose products that minimize the use of plastic and are packaged in glass or metal, which are more easily recycled than most plastics. Additionally, consider the size and amount of packaging used —less is often more, reducing the waste that will eventually need to be disposed of or recycled.

Supporting Small, Local Producers

One of the most impactful ways to ensure sustainability in your skincare routine is to buy from small, local producers. These producers often use traditional methods that are less harmful to the environment and prioritize the quality of their ingredients over mass production. By shopping at local farmers' markets or small online retailers who value sustainable practices, you get fresher, more ethical ingredients and support the local economy. This reduces the carbon footprint of transporting goods long distances, further aligning your skincare routine with eco-friendly practices.

Moreover, small producers are more likely to engage in sustainable farming practices such as crop rotation, organic farming, and non-GMO seeds, which maintain soil health and biodiversity. By supporting these producers, you contribute to preserving traditional farming methods that respect the earth and its natural cycles. This choice benefits your skin and helps maintain a healthy, sustainable environment for future generations.

In this detailed exploration of sustainable shopping practices, you are equipped with the knowledge to make choices that reflect your commitment to personal and planetary health. Each product you select, each brand you support, becomes part of a larger narrative of change, pushing the beauty industry towards more ethical and sustainable practices. Remember that your choices have power as you continue to navigate this complex market. They shape the demand for and supply of sustainable beauty products, forging a path towards a more responsible and conscious approach to skincare.

Farmer's Market to Face: Building Relationships with Local Growers

When you source your skincare ingredients locally, you do more than enhance your beauty regimen; you contribute positively to the local economy and take a stand for environmental sustainability. Local sourcing significantly reduces the carbon footprint of transporting goods over long distances, making this practice a green choice for your skincare routine. Moreover, ingredients obtained from local farms are often fresher and richer in nutrients, providing more potent benefits for your skin. These locally sourced items have not endured long storage periods or extensive travel, which can deplete their natural qualities. By incorporating these fresh, potent ingredients into your skincare, you benefit from their full range of vitamins and antioxidants and support the local economy. This support helps sustain farmers who employ environmentally friendly practices and contributes to community welfare by keeping the local economy robust and vibrant.

Engaging with local farmers opens up a world where you can learn directly about the cultivation practices and the quality of the ingredients you purchase. This interaction fosters a deeper understanding of where your skincare ingredients come from and how they are grown, ensuring they meet your standards for natural and sustainable beauty products. Start by visiting local farmers' markets and speaking directly with the producers. Ask them about their farming methods, whether they use organic practices, chemical pesticides, or fertilizers. Many farmers are proud of their methods and happy to share their knowledge and insights. These conversations can enlighten you about the quality and sustainability of the ingredients you purchase, making your skincare routine a beautifying process and an informed, eco-friendly practice. Building relationships with these farmers often gives you access to custom orders of your favorite items, ensuring you always have access to the freshest ingredients for your skincare creations.

The concept of seasonal skincare is another enriching aspect of sourcing locally. Just as we adjust our diets to include fruits and vegetables that are in season, we can also adapt our skincare routines to use freshly available ingredients.

Seasonal skincare not only aligns with the environment's natural cycles but also optimizes the benefits of fresh ingredients at their peak. For instance, using strawberries rich in vitamin C and antioxidants during the spring can help combat the dullness brought on by winter. In the fall, pumpkin, with its enzymes and alpha hydroxy acids, can be great for a nourishing face mask that exfoliates and brightens the skin. Adapting your skincare routine this way ensures that you are using ingredients that are not only at their most effective but also environmentally sensible choices.

Community-supported agriculture (CSA) programs present a fantastic opportunity to deepen your commitment to local sourcing. By joining a CSA, you receive regular deliveries of farm-fresh products, which ensures a steady supply of fresh, organic ingredients for your skincare needs. This arrangement supports farmers by providing them with predictable income and a guaranteed crop market, which can help them maintain sustainable farming operations. Participating in a CSA also exposes you to a wider variety of ingredients, some of which you might not have chosen otherwise. This variety can inspire creativity in your skincare formulations and introduce you to new, beneficial ingredients that could become staples in your beauty routine. Moreover, CSA programs often foster a sense of community among members, who share recipes, usage tips, and product ideas, enriching your experience and knowledge in natural skincare.

By embracing sourcing locally, building relationships with growers, adapting to seasonal skincare, and participating in CSA programs, you actively contribute to a culture of sustainability and support for local economies. This approach benefits your skin and personal health and promotes a healthier planet and community. As you continue exploring the benefits of close-to-home ingredients, remember that each choice you make at the farmer's market or with your CSA shapes your beauty routine and the world around you.

The Zero-Waste Beauty Kitchen: Minimizing Skincare's Footprint

Embracing a zero-waste lifestyle in your skincare routine isn't just about reducing waste; it's a holistic approach that involves rethinking how we consume and what we do with the byproducts of our daily regimens. The principles of zero-waste skincare— reduction, reuse, and recycling—are vital in creating a routine that respects our bodies and the planet. Reduction focuses on decreasing the waste we produce, beginning with selecting products that come in minimal or eco-friendly packaging. Reuse involves finding new ways to use old products, such as repurposing glass jars as containers for homemade skincare. Recycling should be considered a last resort and involves processing items to make them functional again, ensuring materials like plastic and glass don't end up in landfills.

In the spirit of reuse, let's explore how you can incorporate DIY reusable skincare tools into your routine, significantly cutting down on waste. For instance, consider using washable cloth pads instead of disposable makeup wipes. These can be made from soft, natural fabrics like bamboo or cotton, which are gentle on the skin and can be washed and reused often. Crafting your washcloths or buying sustainably made options replaces the need for single-use alternatives. Similarly, instead of disposable applicators, opt for sustainable materials such as bamboo or recycled plastic, which can be washed and reused. Even your skincare mixtures can be stored in glass jars or bottles you've saved from other products, reducing the need for new plastic containers.

Minimizing waste when sourcing ingredients for homemade skin care products is crucial in maintaining a zero-waste regimen. One effective strategy is buying in bulk, which often reduces the amount of packaging needed and can decrease overall waste. Look for stores or suppliers that offer ingredients like clays, oils, and dried herbs in bulk, allowing you to purchase only the amount you need and, often, at a reduced price. Moreover, choosing products that come with minimal packaging— or packaging that has been made from recycled materials—is crucial. When shopping, carry reusable bags or containers to avoid unnecessary plastic bags. These small changes in how you shop for your skincare ingredients can profoundly impact your waste output.

Lastly, the practices of composting and repurposing leftovers from your skincare preparations not only help reduce waste but also enrich your environment. Many natural skincare ingredients, such as coffee grounds, eggshells, and fruit peels, can be composted after use, contributing to a nutrient-rich compost that can be used to nourish your garden. This helps reduce the amount of organic waste going to landfills and supports a sustainable cycle of growth and renewal in your backyard. Additionally, some leftovers from skincare products can be creatively repurposed. For example, leftover herbal infusions can water plants, providing them with added nutrients or repurposed as hair rinses. Implementing these practices allows you to step closer to a zero-waste lifestyle, where every item is utilized to its fullest potential, and nothing is seen as mere waste.

Your skincare routine can become a testament to

sustainable living through these efforts in reducing, reusing, and recycling, combined with thoughtful purchasing and creative repurposing. Each choice to minimize waste contributes to your skin's health and supports a more significant commitment to protecting and nurturing the environment. By adopting a zero-waste approach, you become part of a movement that values sustainability, resourcefulness, and respect for the natural world, embodying the principles of a genuinely holistic skincare practice that cares for both the self and the planet.

Upcycling for Beauty: Creative Containers and Storage Solutions

In the spirit of sustainability and creativity, upcycling old containers gives them a new lease of life and adds a personalized touch to your skincare regimen. Imagine transforming an old, ornate jam jar into a container for your homemade lavender face cream or repurposing a brightly colored tea tin as a holder for your natural lip balms. The possibilities for repurposing are as limitless as your imagination. Start by gathering old skincare containers or any attractive jars, bottles, or boxes you might usually discard. Clean them thoroughly to remove all residues of their former contents, which is particularly important to prevent unwanted reactions with your new skincare products. Sterilizing glass containers in boiling water can ensure they are spotless and safe for reuse.

Creativity in decorating these containers can significantly enhance your skincare experience. Personalizing your skincare packaging isn't just about aesthetics; it's about creating a product that feels uniquely yours, one that you're excited to reach for in your daily routine. Use non-toxic paints, adhesive decorations, or even fabric to add color and texture to the containers. For instance, wrapping a glass jar in burlap and securing it with a pretty ribbon can give it a rustic charm, or painting the lid of a tin container with chalkboard paint allows for customizable and erasable labeling. These small artistic projects breathe new life into old containers and make using the products inside more enjoyable.

When choosing containers for storing homemade skincare products, it's crucial to consider the safety and effectiveness of the product over time. Certain ingredients in skincare products, particularly natural and preservative-free ones, can be sensitive to light and air exposure, affecting their stability and efficacy. Dark glass bottles can help shield light-sensitive ingredients like essential oils from sunlight, while airtight containers can prevent the oxidation of products such as vitamin C serums. Always consider the specific requirements of the skincare product when selecting an upcycled container to ensure it maintains its beneficial properties for as long as possible.

Organizing your DIY skincare products efficiently ensures they are easy to access and use, making your beauty routine smooth and enjoyable. Designate a space in your bathroom or vanity for your skincare products and arrange them in a way that makes sense for your routine. Use stands, spice racks, or small shelves to keep the containers organized and within easy reach. Labeling each container helps avoid confusion and ensures you use the right product for your skin's needs. Consider using a small, dedicated beauty fridge for products that need to be kept cool, such as specific face masks or creams. This helps maintain the potency of the products and adds a feeling of luxury to your skincare routine, making each use a refreshing experience.

In this exploration of upcycling for beauty, we've seen how repurposing old containers and personalizing them can trans- form your approach to skincare storage, making it more sustainable, enjoyable, and tailored to your style. Upcycling reduces waste and enhances your connection to your skincare routine, encouraging a deeper engagement with the products you use and how you use them. By choosing to upcycle, you are deciding to support the environment while adding beauty and organization to your daily skincare practice.

Ending Note

This chapter delved into the innovative and eco-friendly practice of upcycling in the context of beauty and skincare. By creatively repurposing old containers, not only do we reduce waste, but we also add a personalized charm to our skincare routines. This approach aligns with the broader sustainability and mindful consumption themes explored in previous chapters. As we transition to the next chapter, we will continue to build on these foundational ideas, exploring more ways to integrate holistic and sustainable practices into our everyday lives, thereby enhancing both our well-being and the health of our planet.

Chapter 5: The Art of the Face Mask

In the lush skincare landscape, the humble face mask stands out not just as a remedy but as a ritual, offering a unique blend of nurturing and transformation that touches our skin and spirits. Just as a painter selects the perfect palette to create a masterpiece, crafting a face mask requires a discerning selection of ingredients, each chosen for its unique benefits and harmonious interaction. This chapter is your guide to unlocking the secrets of these magical concoctions, turning everyday ingredients into potions that rejuvenate, cleanse, and illuminate your complexion.

Face Mask Fundamentals: The Base Recipes

Introduction to Base Recipes

At the heart of every effective face mask is a well-crafted base. This foundational mixture is the canvas upon which your skin's transformation occurs. Whether your skin craves hydration, seeks clarity, or needs a touch of brightness, each base recipe is designed to target specific needs. From the creamy, moisture-rich bases perfect for dry or winter-beaten skin to the light, clarifying bases that address oiliness and impurities, the suitable base sets the stage for the following active ingredients.

Ingredient Selection and Benefits

Choosing the right facial mask ingredients is akin to selecting the finest spices for a gourmet meal. Each ingredient is selected for its primary function and ability to synergize with others. Natural yogurt or honey are paramount for hydration due to their intense moisturizing properties and richness in skin-friendly bacteria or enzymes. Green clay or activated charcoal are favorites for cleansing, known for their ability to draw out impurities and detoxify the skin without stripping it of natural oils. To brighten the skin, ingredients like fresh lemon juice or turmeric are incorporated for their natural astringent properties and high vitamin C content, which aids in lightening discoloration and enhancing the skin's natural glow.

Step-by-step Mixing Process

Creating your face mask is a ritual in its own right, involving carefully blending components to achieve the perfect consistency and potency. Begin by measuring your base ingredients, ensuring they are fresh and high-quality. If you're using dry ingredients like clay or powdered herbs, sift them to avoid clumps that can make the application uneven. Wet ingredients should be at room temperature to ensure they mix well. Combine the base ingredients gently until they form a smooth, homogenous mixture. Gradually add secondary ingredients like essential oils or vitamin serums, stirring continuously to distribute them evenly throughout the mixture. This methodical mixing ensures that each face mask portion is potent and effective.

Application and Removal Techniques

The application of a face mask is a moment of connection between you and your skin. Start with a clean, slightly damp face, which helps the mask adhere better and allows for easier absorption of the ingredients. Using your fingertips or a soft brush, apply the mask in a gentle, circular motion, starting from the cheeks and moving toward the outer edges of your face. Avoid the delicate areas around your eyes and mouth. Allow the mask to sit for the prescribed period, which ranges from 10 to 20 minutes, depending on the ingredients' intensity.

Removing the facemask is just as important as applying it. Use lukewarm water and a soft washcloth, rinsing gently and circularly to lift and remove the mask without pulling at the skin. Finish with a splash of cool water to close your pores, and pat your face gently with a towel to dry. This method ensures that your skin reaps all the mask's benefits without experiencing stress or irritation during removal.

Mastering these fundamental recipes and techniques sets the stage for more advanced customizations and innovations in your skincare routine. Each mask you create brings you closer to achieving your desired skin condition and deepens your understanding of how natural ingredients can be transformed into powerful tools for beauty and wellness. As you continue experimenting and learning, remember that each face mask reflects your skincare journey and is tailored to meet your evolving skin's unique needs and aspirations.

Customization 101: Tailoring Your Mask to Your Skin Type

Understanding your skin type is the first essential step in crafting a face mask that not only feels good but also addresses your specific skin concerns. Skin types vary widely, from dry, which may feel tight and show flaking, to oily, characterized by a glossy shine and larger pores. Then there's combination skin, which features elements of dry and oily types across different face areas, and sensitive skin, which tends to react with redness or irritation to new products or ingredients. Lastly, acne-prone skin, susceptible to breakouts, requires careful handling and specific ingredients to help manage and prevent acne effectively.

A simple observation method after cleansing can be quite telling when determining your skin type. Wash your face with a gentle cleanser and pat it dry. After about 30 minutes, observe how your skin feels. If it feels tight or shows flaky patches, it's likely dry. Your skin is oily if there's a noticeable shine on your forehead, nose, and chin. If only certain areas like your T-zone (forehead, nose, and chin) are shiny, you probably have combination skin. It may be sensitive if your skin feels uncomfortable, red, or itchy. Understanding these characteristics helps you select the right ingredients to harmonize with your skin rather than aggravate it.

Once you've identified your skin type, tailoring your face mask involves choosing ingredients that enhance the health and appearance of your skin. For dry skin, ingredients that offer deep hydration and nourishment are key. Consider incorporating natural oils like avocado or almond oil, which provide intense moisture and help restore the skin's barrier. Hyaluronic acid, a powerhouse hydrator, can also be beneficial, pulling moisture into the skin to plump and alleviate dryness. On the other hand, oily skin benefits from ingredients that can help regulate sebum production without over-drying. Green and kaolin clay are excellent for absorbing excess oil and purifying pores. Adding a bit of witch hazel can provide astringent properties to tighten pores and refine skin texture.

Combination skin requires a balanced approach, using ingrdients that address oiliness and dryness. Combining jojoba oil, which balances oil production, and cucumber, which hydrates and soothes, can work wonders. Sensitive skin, meanwhile, will thrive with soothing ingredients like oatmeal and aloe vera, which calm irritation and reduce redness. Incorporating antibacterial and anti-inflammatory ingredients like tea tree oil and honey can help treat breakouts and prevent new ones from forming for those dealing with acne-prone skin.

Adjusting your base recipes to cater to specific skin concerns such as redness, acne, or hyperpigmentation involves more than just picking the right ingredients; it's about understanding how these components interact with each other and your skin. For instance, if combating hyperpigmentation, a face mask with lemon juice might be effective for its natural brightening properties. However, lemon juice should be diluted appropriately and not used too frequently, as its high acidity can irritate the skin. Pairing it with a soothing ingredient like honey or yogurt can mitigate potential irritation while amplifying the mask's skin-brightening effects.

Encouraging experimentation and adjustment in your face mask formulations allows for a truly personalized skincare experience. It's essential to listen to your skin's responses after each application. If a mask leaves your skin feeling overly tight or uncomfortable, consider reducing harsh ingredients or increasing soothing or hydrating components.

Conversely, if you're not seeing the desired effect, it might be time to improve the potency of active ingredients or adjust their ratios. Remember, the goal is to create a face mask that feels good when applied and leaves your skin feeling better. By embracing a trial-and-error approach, you can refine your masks to meet your skin's evolving needs better, ensuring each application brings you closer to your ideal skin health and appearance.

The Quick Fix: Facemasks for Busy Lifestyles

In the whirlwind of daily responsibilities, finding moments for self-care, particularly for elaborate skincare routines, can often feel like a luxury that time doesn't allow. However, maintaining glowing, healthy skin doesn't have to be sidelined due to a packed schedule. The secret lies in integrating efficient skincare practices that align with your busy lifestyle, transforming necessity into convenience. For those of you constantly on the go, quick and effective face masks, which require minimal time without compromising benefits, can be a game-changer in your skincare regimen.

Regarding time-saving tips, the art of pre-preparation must be balanced. Like meal prepping for the week, you can prepare multiple batches of your favorite face mask recipes during your downtime. Use natural preservatives like Vitamin E or certain essential oils to extend their freshness, and store them in airtight containers in the refrigerator. This ensures that your masks retain their potency and that you have a ready-to-apply skincare treatment at your fingertips. Consider also the formulation of your masks; ingredients like clay or oats can be pre-mixed dry and then quickly blended with water or honey when ready for application. This method reduces preparation time to just a few minutes, making it easier to fit into a hectic morning or evening routine.

Multi-tasking masks offer another strategic avenue for those balancing tight schedules. These formulations simultaneously provide multiple skincare benefits, such as deep cleansing while hydrating or offering exfoliation alongside nourishment. Ingredients such as yogurt, which moisturizes and gently exfoliates due to its lactic acid content, or honey, known for its antibacterial properties and hydrating benefits, make excellent bases. Adding green tea powder can further enhance these masks due to its antioxidant properties, which help fight signs of aging and soothe inflamed or sensitive skin. By applying a multi-tasking mask, you streamline your skincare routine without cutting corners on the quality of your skincare.

Incorporating face masks into your existing routine can also streamline your skincare process. Consider applying a face mask during a morning shower. The steam helps to open up your pores, allowing the mask's nutrients to penetrate more deeply. A mask can work magic on your skin while you do other shower tasks, such as shampooing or conditioning your hair. This integration not only saves time but also enhances the mask's effectiveness. Similarly, applying a face mask while answering emails or preparing your morning coffee can turn a mundane task into a moment of pampering. It's about finding those small gaps in your routine where a facemask can be included without feeling like an additional task.

Lastly, quick clean-up is crucial for those with limited time. Face masks that rinse off easily with water, without repeated washing or scrubbing, are ideal. Masks based on gel or light cream bases can be more convenient than heavy, clay-based masks, which might require more effort to remove altogether.

After rinsing, a quick swipe with a toner-soaked cotton pad can ensure that any residual mask is removed, leaving your skin fresh and clear. Opting for no-wash, leave-on masks that absorb into the skin and require no rinsing can also be a practical option for nighttime routines, allowing the active ingredients to work as you sleep.

Adapting these strategies allows your skincare regimen to remain robust without demanding substantial time investments. Face masks, often seen as a pampering luxury, can be seamlessly integrated into the busiest schedules with some planning and the proper techniques. This approach keeps your skin in optimal condition and ensures that your skincare routine is a source of relaxation and rejuvenation rather than a time-consuming chore.

Seasonal Skincare: Masks for Every Climate and Season

As the seasons shift, bringing changes in weather and environmental conditions, your skin undergoes its own transformations. The varying humidity, temperature, and exposure to elements like wind and sun can significantly affect skin health. Adapting your face mask regimen to align with seasonal needs is crucial to keep your skin radiant and resilient through these transitions. This ensures your skin is getting the right kind of care at the right time and optimizes the efficacy of the natural ingredients used in your masks.

During the chilly, dry winter months, the air becomes harsh and stripped of moisture, often leaving skin feeling dry and sensitive. Face masks focusing on hydration and barrier protection are your best allies to counteract this. Ingredients like hyaluronic acid, which can hold up to 1000 times its weight in water, become invaluable for their intense moisture-retaining properties. Combining this with rich, nourishing oils such as argan or evening primrose oil provides a double action effect— moisturizing the skin while forming a protective layer that locks in moisture and shields the skin from biting winds and indoor heating. A simple yet effective winter mask can be made by mixing high-grade hyaluronic acid serum with aloe vera gel, a soothing agent, and a few drops of argan oil for an extra layer of protection. Apply this mask in the evening, allowing it to work overnight so you wake up to replenished and supple skin.

As the seasons turn and summer comes into full swing, the focus shifts from protection against the cold to cooling and soothing skin exposed to the sun. Ingredients with cooling properties, like cucumber and aloe vera, are perfect for summer face masks. They provide a refreshing relief and help soothe sunburnt or heat-irritated skin. Antioxidants are also crucial during this season to combat the increased exposure to UV rays, which can accelerate skin aging. With its high antioxidant content, green tea can be incorporated into face masks to help mitigate this damage. A revitalizing summer mask recipe might include pureed cucumber, aloe vera gel, and green tea powder. This mixture not only cools and calms the skin but also works to repair and protect it from photo-aging.

Transitioning between seasons can sometimes be challenging for your skin, often leading to imbalances as it adjusts to new environmental conditions. This makes the transitional periods an ideal time to focus on balancing and normalizing skin functions. Face masks during this time should be designed to gently adapt your skin to upcoming conditions while correcting any imbalances that might have occurred in the previous season. For instance, as you move from winter to spring, gradually introducing lighter moisturizing ingredients and incorporating gentle exfoliants can help wake up and prepare the skin for higher humidity levels. A transitional face mask might include ingredients like honey, known for its humectant properties, combined with fine oatmeal, which gently exfoliates without stripping the skin of its natural oils.

Understanding and adapting to your skin's specific needs with each changing season ensures that your skincare regimen remains dynamic and responsive. This proactive approach optimizes your skin year-round and enhances your connection to the environment's natural cycles. As you learn to listen to your skin and respond with the appropriate seasonal care, your skincare routine evolves into a more mindful and attuned practice, reflecting the changing landscapes around you.

In summary, this exploration into seasonal skincare under-scores the importance of attuning your skincare routine to the rhythmic changes of the environment. Each season dictates a specific approach to skin health, from the deep hydration needed in winter to the soothing coolness required in summer. By adapting your face mask ingredients and formulations to these needs, you enhance your skincare routine's effectiveness and engage in a deeper, more harmonious relationship with the natural world. The next chapter will build on these foundational practices as we move forward, introducing more advanced techniques and recipes to refine and enhance your skincare regimen, ensuring it remains as dynamic and vibrant as the world around you.

Chapter 6: More Natural Face Mask Recipes

These natural and nontoxic face mask recipes using common household products and food offer a variety of natural ingredients that can help to nourish and rejuvenate your skin without the use of harsh chemicals. For additional recipes, you can explore various combinations of these and other natural ingredients to create your own personalized face masks.

1. Avocado and Honey Mask

- **Ingredients**: 1/2 avocado, 1 tablespoon honey
- **Directions**: Mash avocado and mix with honey. Apply to face, leave for 15 minutes, and rinse off with warm water.

2. Oatmeal and Yogurt Mask

· **Ingredients**: 2 tablespoons oatmeal, 1 tablespoon yogurt, 1 teaspoon honey
· **Directions**: Mix oatmeal, yogurt, and honey. Apply to face, leave for 15 minutes, and rinse off with warm water.

3. Banana and Honey Mask

· **Ingredients**: 1/2 banana, 1 tablespoon honey
· **Directions**: Mash banana and mix with honey. Apply to face, leave for 15 minutes, and rinse off with warm water.

4. Coffee and Coconut Oil Mask

· **Ingredients**: 2 tablespoons coffee grounds, 1 tablespoon coconut oil
· **Directions**: Mix coffee grounds with coconut oil. Apply to face, leave for 10 minutes, and rinse off with warm water.

5. Cucumber and Aloe Vera Mask

· **Ingredients**: 1/2 cucumber, 2 tablespoons aloe vera gel
· **Directions**: Blend cucumber and mix with aloe vera gel. Apply to face, leave for 15 minutes, and rinse off with cool water.

6. Egg White and Lemon Mask

· **Ingredients**: 1 egg white, 1 teaspoon lemon juice
· **Directions**: Beat egg white until foamy and mix with lemon juice. Apply to face, leave for 10 minutes, and rinse off with warm water.

7. Honey and Lemon Mask

· **Ingredients**: 1 tablespoon honey, 1 teaspoon lemon juice
· **Directions**: Mix honey and lemon juice. Apply to face, leave for 15 minutes, and rinse off with warm water.

8. Papaya and Honey Mask

· **Ingredients**: 1/2 cup mashed papaya, 1 tablespoon honey
· **Directions**: Mix papaya and honey. Apply to face, leave for 15 minutes, and rinse off with warm water.

9. Strawberry and Yogurt Mask

- **Ingredients**: 3 strawberries, 1 tablespoon yogurt
- **Directions**: Mash strawberries and mix with yogurt. Apply to face, leave for 15 minutes, and rinse off with warm water.

10. Turmeric and Yogurt Mask

- **Ingredients**: 1 teaspoon turmeric, 2 tablespoons yogurt
- **Directions**: Mix turmeric and yogurt. Apply to face, leave for 15 minutes, and rinse off with warm water.

11. Cocoa and Milk Mask

- **Ingredients**: 1 tablespoon cocoa powder, 2 tablespoons milk
- **Directions**: Mix cocoa powder and milk. Apply to face, leave for 15 minutes, and rinse off with warm water.

12. Baking Soda and Water Mask

- **Ingredients**: 1 tablespoon baking soda, 1 tablespoon water
- **Directions**: Mix baking soda and water. Apply to face, leave for 10 minutes, and rinse off with warm water.

13. Green Tea and Honey Mask

· **Ingredients**: 1 tablespoon green tea leaves, 1 tablespoon honey
· **Directions**: Mix green tea leaves and honey. Apply to face, leave for 15 minutes, and rinse off with warm water.

14. Yogurt and Lemon Mask

· **Ingredients**: 2 tablespoons yogurt, 1 teaspoon lemon juice
· **Directions**: Mix yogurt and lemon juice. Apply to face, leave for 15 minutes, and rinse off with warm water.

15. Milk and Honey Mask

· **Ingredients**: 2 tablespoons milk, 1 tablespoon honey
· **Directions**: Mix milk and honey. Apply to face, leave for 15 minutes, and rinse off with warm water.

16. Cucumber and Oatmeal Mask

· **Ingredients**: 1/2 cucumber, 2 tablespoons oatmeal
· **Directions**: Blend cucumber and mix with oatmeal. Apply to face, leave for 15 minutes, and rinse off with cool water.

17. Apple and Honey Mask

· **Ingredients**: 1/2 apple, 1 tablespoon honey
· **Directions**: Mash apple and mix with honey. Apply to face, leave for 15 minutes, and rinse off with warm water.

18. Pumpkin and Honey Mask

· **Ingredients**: 2 tablespoons pumpkin puree, 1 tablespoon honey
· **Directions**: Mix pumpkin puree and honey. Apply to face, leave for 15 minutes, and rinse off with warm water.

19. Aloe Vera and Honey Mask

· **Ingredients**: 2 tablespoons aloe vera gel, 1 tablespoon honey
· **Directions**: Mix aloe vera gel and honey. Apply to face, leave for 15 minutes, and rinse off with cool water.

20. Rose Water and Sandalwood Mask

· **Ingredients**: 2 tablespoons sandalwood powder, 1 table-spoon rose water
· **Directions**: Mix sandalwood powder and rose water. Apply to face, leave for 15 minutes, and rinse off with cool water.

21. Tomato and Sugar Mask

· **Ingredients**: 1 ripe tomato, 2 tablespoons sugar
· **Directions**: Blend tomato and mix with sugar. Apply to face, leave for 10 minutes, and rinse off with cool water.

22. Rice Flour and Milk Mask

· **Ingredients**: 2 tablespoons rice flour, 2 tablespoons milk
· **Directions**: Mix rice flour and milk. Apply to face, leave for 15 minutes, and rinse off with warm water.

23. Honey and Cinnamon Mask

· **Ingredients**: 1 tablespoon honey, 1 teaspoon cinnamon
· **Directions**: Mix honey and cinnamon. Apply to face, leave for 10 minutes, and rinse off with warm water.

24. Lemon and Sugar Mask

· **Ingredients**: 1 tablespoon lemon juice, 2 tablespoons sugar
· **Directions**: Mix lemon juice and sugar. Apply to face, leave for 10 minutes, and rinse off with warm water.

25. Aloe Vera and Turmeric Mask

· **Ingredients**: 2 tablespoons aloe vera gel, 1 teaspoon turmeric
· **Directions**: Mix aloe vera gel and turmeric. Apply to face, leave for 15 minutes, and rinse off with cool water.

26. Mint and Honey Mask

· **Ingredients**: 10 fresh mint leaves, 1 tablespoon honey
· **Directions**: Crush mint leaves and mix with honey. Apply to face, leave for 15 minutes, and rinse off with cool water.

27. Cucumber and Yogurt Mask

· **Ingredients**: 1/2 cucumber, 2 tablespoons yogurt
· **Directions**: Blend cucumber and mix with yogurt. Apply to face, leave for 15 minutes, and rinse off with cool water.

28. Baking Soda and Lemon Mask

· **Ingredients**: 1 tablespoon baking soda, 1 tablespoon lemon juice
· **Directions**: Mix baking soda and lemon juice. Apply to face, leave for 10 minutes, and rinse off with warm water.

29. Coconut Oil and Honey Mask

- **Ingredients**: 1 tablespoon coconut oil, 1 tablespoon honey
- **Directions**: Mix coconut oil and honey. Apply to face, leave for 15 minutes, and rinse off with warm water.

30. Honey and Apple Cider Vinegar Mask

- **Ingredients**: 1 tablespoon honey, 1 teaspoon apple cider vinegar
- **Directions**: Mix honey and apple cider vinegar. Apply to face, leave for 10 minutes, and rinse off with warm water.

31. Carrot and Honey Mask

- **Ingredients**: 1 cooked carrot, 1 tablespoon honey
- **Directions**: Mash carrot and mix with honey. Apply to face, leave for 15 minutes, and rinse off with warm water.

32. Green Tea and Lemon Mask

- **Ingredients**: 1 tablespoon green tea leaves, 1 teaspoon lemon juice
- **Directions**: Mix green tea leaves and lemon juice. Apply to face, leave for 15 minutes, and rinse off with cool water.

33. Coconut Milk and Honey Mask

· **Ingredients**: 2 tablespoons coconut milk, 1 tablespoon honey
· **Directions**: Mix coconut milk and honey. Apply to face, leave for 15 minutes, and rinse off with warm water.

34. Potato and Lemon Mask

· **Ingredients**: 1 small potato, 1 teaspoon lemon juice
· **Directions**: Grate potato and mix with lemon juice. Apply to face, leave for 15 minutes, and rinse off with cool water.

35. Papaya and Yogurt Mask

· **Ingredients**: 1/2 cup mashed papaya, 2 tablespoons yogurt
· **Directions**: Mix papaya and yogurt. Apply to face, leave for 15 minutes, and rinse off with warm water.

36. Oatmeal and Banana Mask

· **Ingredients**: 2 tablespoons oatmeal, 1/2 banana
· **Directions**: Mash banana and mix with oatmeal. Apply to face, leave for 15 minutes, and rinse off with warm water.

37. Rose Water and Glycerin Mask

· **Ingredients**: 2 tablespoons rose water, 1 tablespoon glycerin
· **Directions**: Mix rose water and glycerin. Apply to face, leave for 15 minutes, and rinse off with cool water.

38. Almond and Milk Mask

· **Ingredients**: 1 tablespoon almond powder, 2 tablespoons milk
· **Directions**: Mix almond powder and milk. Apply to face, leave for 15 minutes, and rinse off with warm water.

39. Pumpkin and Coconut Oil Mask

· **Ingredients**: 2 tablespoons pumpkin puree, 1 tablespoon coconut oil
· **Directions**: Mix pumpkin puree and coconut oil. Apply to face, leave for 15 minutes, and rinse off with warm water.

40. Strawberry and Honey Mask

· **Ingredients**: 3 strawberries, 1 tablespoon honey
· **Directions**: Mash strawberries and mix with honey. Apply to face, leave for 15 minutes, and rinse off with warm water.

41. Avocado and Yogurt Mask

· **Ingredients**: 1/2 avocado, 2 tablespoons yogurt
· **Directions**: Mash avocado and mix with yogurt. Apply to face, leave for 15 minutes, and rinse off with warm water.

42. Honey and Rose Water Mask

· **Ingredients**: 1 tablespoon honey, 1 tablespoon rose water
· **Directions**: Mix honey and rose water. Apply to face, leave for 15 minutes, and rinse off with warm water.

43. Baking Soda and Honey Mask

· **Ingredients**: 1 tablespoon baking soda, 1 tablespoon honey
· **Directions**: Mix baking soda and honey. Apply to face, leave for 10 minutes, and rinse off with warm water.

44. Cucumber and Mint Mask

· **Ingredients**: 1/2 cucumber, 10 fresh mint leaves
· **Directions**: Blend cucumber and mint leaves. Apply to face, leave for 15 minutes, and rinse off with cool water.

45. Turmeric and Honey Mask

· **Ingredients**: 1 teaspoon turmeric, 1 tablespoon honey
· **Directions**: Mix turmeric and honey. Apply to face, leave for 15 minutes, and rinse off with warm water.

46. Green Tea and Aloe Vera Mask

· **Ingredients**: 1 tablespoon green tea leaves, 2 tablespoons aloe vera gel
· **Directions**: Mix green tea leaves and aloe vera gel. Apply to face, leave for 15 minutes, and rinse off with cool water.

47. Apple and Oatmeal Mask

· **Ingredients**: 1/2 apple, 2 tablespoons oatmeal
· **Directions**: Grate apple and mix with oatmeal. Apply to face, leave for 15 minutes, and rinse off with warm water.

48. Honey and Yogurt Mask

· **Ingredients**: 1 tablespoon honey, 2 tablespoons yogurt
· **Directions**: Mix honey and yogurt. Apply to face, leave for 15 minutes, and rinse off with warm water.

49. Potato and Honey Mask

· **Ingredients**: 1 small potato, 1 tablespoon honey
· **Directions**: Grate potato and mix with honey. Apply to face, leave for 15 minutes, and rinse off with warm water.

50. Coconut Milk and Almond Mask

· **Ingredients**: 2 tablespoons coconut milk, 1 tablespoon almond powder
· **Directions**: Mix coconut milk and almond powder. Apply to face, leave for 15 minutes, and rinse off with warm water.

Unwind with these delightful homemade recipes for a relaxing evening, or bring your friends together for a cozy night in and organize a fun and rejuvenating face mask party!

Chapter 7: Beyond Face Masks

As you delve deeper into natural skincare, the journey expands beyond the soothing layers of facemasks into the stimulating world of scrubs and the protective embrace of balms. These essential skincare staples do more than complement your face mask rituals; they are pivotal in enhancing your skin's health, texture, and resilience. Imagine standing at the edge of a serene ocean, the waves gently polishing the pebbles on the shore. Similarly, natural scrubs and balms work in tandem to refine and fortify your skin, leaving it as smooth and radiant as sea- polished stones.

Scrubs and Balms: Exfoliating and Moisturizing Naturally

Homemade Scrubs for Gentle Exfoliation

The secret to maintaining vibrant, healthy skin lies in the art of exfoliation. By gently removing dead skin cells, scrubs help reveal the fresh, glowing skin underneath. However, the key is to use gentle ingredients that do not damage or irritate your skin. Natural exfoliants like sugar, salt, and oatmeal are perfect for this purpose, each offering a unique benefit tailored to different skin types. Sugar granules, for instance, are small and smooth, making them ideal for sensitive skin types. They not only exfoliate but also contain glycolic acid, which helps to break down dead skin cells and support cell turnover naturally. Salt, with its mineral-rich profile, is excellent for more resilient skin types, providing a deeper exfoliation and helping to cleanse pores deeply. Oatmeal, known for its soothing properties, is perfect for those with dry or reactive skin, as it gently exfoliates while calming the skin.

Creating a customized scrub that caters to your skin needs can transform your skincare routine. Mix finely ground oatmeal with honey and a touch of almond oil for a hydrating and soothing scrub. The oatmeal gently exfoliates, the honey hydrates and offers antibacterial properties, and the almond oil nourishes the skin, leaving it soft and supple. For those seeking a more invigorating scrub, combine coarse sea salt with coconut oil and a few drops of peppermint essential oil for a refreshing, revitalizing experience. The salt cleanses and exfoliates, the coconut oil moisturizes, and the peppermint oil refreshes the skin and the senses.

Creating Nourishing Balms

Transitioning from scrubs to balms, the focus shifts from exfoliation to deep, lasting hydration and protection. Balms are concentrated, healing ointments that moisturize the skin and create a protective barrier that locks in moisture and shields the skin from environmental stressors. Crafting a balm that suits your skin type involves selecting the right combination of natural oils, butter, and waxes to achieve a formula that melts into your skin, providing hydration and nourishment.

For a simple yet effective balm, start with shea butter, known for its deep moisturizing properties and rich content of vitamins A and E. Melt the shea butter in a double boiler and mix it with jojoba oil, which is light and easily absorbed, making it suitable for all skin types. Add beeswax to thicken the mixture and form a protective layer on the skin. For added benefits, consider incorporating essential oils like lavender for soothing or tea tree for its antibacterial properties, depending on your skin's needs. Pour the mixture into a clean container and let it solidify. This balm can be used on the lips, face, and body, providing a versatile, all-in-one solution for dryness and discomfort.

Benefits of Regular Exfoliation and Moisturization

Incorporating regular exfoliation and moisturization into your skincare routine is crucial for maintaining healthy, glowing skin. Exfoliation removes the barrier of dead skin cells clogging the skin and uncovers fresh new cells below. This opens the way for moisturizing products to penetrate more deeply into the skin, making them more effective. Regular moisturization keeps the skin hydrated, supple, and protected from environmental factors that can cause dryness and irritation. Together, these practices help maintain the skin's integrity, prevent signs of aging, and ensure your skin remains vibrant and resilient.

Customization Tips for Scrubs and Balms

Customizing your scrubs and balms allows you to address your unique skin concerns and preferences effectively. When creating scrubs, consider the granularity of your chosen exfoliants and your skin's sensitivity. Finer grains offer a gentler exfoliation suitable for the face or sensitive skin, while coarser grains can be ideal for body scrubs. The ratio of oils to waxes for balms can be adjusted depending on the desired consistency and absorption rate. More wax creates a firmer, more protective balm, while more oil produces a softer, nourishing balm.

Adding essential oils can also tailor your products to your sensory preferences and skin benefits. For instance, adding a few drops of chamomile essential oil can enhance the soothing properties of a balm, making it ideal for irritated or sensitive skin. Experimenting with different combinations of oils, butter, and essential oils allows you to create a product ideally suited to your needs. It adds an element of personalization and enjoyment to your skincare routine.

In exploring natural scrubs and balms, we've uncovered the transformative effects of gentle exfoliation and deep moisturization. By understanding the properties of natural exfoliants and moisturizers and learning how to combine them effectively, you can enhance your skincare regimen, ensuring your skin remains polished, nourished, and radiant. As you continue to experiment with these recipes and techniques, remember that each addition or adjustment is a step towards perfecting your skincare ritual, reflecting your unique skin needs and lifestyle.

Toners and Mists: Refreshing and Revitalizing Recipes

In the expansive universe of skincare, toners and mists play pivotal roles that often go unnoticed yet are crucial for maintaining the health and vitality of your skin. Think of toners as the unsung heroes that restore your skin's pH balance after cleansing, preparing it for the subsequent layers of skincare products. A well-formulated toner can remove any residual impurities, balance your skin's pH, and provide an initial layer of hydration, making any moisturizers or treatments you apply afterward more effective. On the other hand, mists are like your skin's personal hydration stations—ready to refresh, soothe, and hydrate your skin at a moment's notice. They are perfect or a midday pick-me-up for for setting makeup, and they can be infused with ingredients that target specific skin concerns like dryness or dullness.

Creating natural toners and mists allows you to tailor ingredients to suit your skin's needs without the harsh chemicals often found in commercial products. Witch hazel offers an excellent foundation for an essential yet effective toner due to its natural astringent properties, which help tighten the pores and smooth the skin. It's particularly beneficial for those with oily or acne-prone skin. To enhance witch hazel's benefits, consider adding rosewater, known for its calming and anti-inflammatory properties, making it ideal for soothing irritated or sensitive skin. Aloe vera gel can be mixed into your formulation for an added hydration boost. This simple combination can significantly improve your skin's tone and texture when used regularly after cleansing.

Incorporating ingredients like green tea and vitamin C can be transformative for those who want a toner that also brightens and revitalizes the skin. Brew a strong cup of green tea, known for its antioxidant properties, and mix it with a small amount of vitamin C powder. This concoction helps protect the skin from environmental damage and brightens the complexion over time. When applying any homemade toner, use a cotton pad to gently swipe over cleansed skin, or pour it into a spray bottle and mist directly onto the face for a more refreshing experience.

Switching focus to facial mists, these delightful concoctions are perfect for keeping your skin hydrated throughout the day. For a hydrating mist, start with a base of distilled water or herbal tea such as chamomile or lavender, which are gentle and soothing. Add glycerin, a humectant that draws moisture into the skin, keeping it hydrated longer. Suppose you want to make the mist more refreshing, especially during the warmer months. In that case, cucumber juice or peppermint essential oil can provide a cooling effect, leaving your skin feeling refreshed and revitalized. These mists can be spritzed on your face throughout the day over makeup or bare skin, providing an instant boost of hydration and refreshment.

Packaging and Preservation Tips

When it comes to storing your homemade toners and mists, choosing the proper packaging is as important as the ingredients inside. Glass bottles are preferred over plastic as they do not react with the ingredients and can help prolong the shelf life of your products. Dark-colored glass bottles are handy for storing products that contain light-sensitive ingredients like essential oils. These bottles can prevent the degradation of the active ingredients, ensuring your toners and mists remain effective for longer.

Preserving homemade skincare products naturally can be challenging, as they lack the strong preservatives found in commercial products. To naturally extend the shelf life of your toners and mists, consider adding natural preservatives such as grapefruit seed extract or rosemary antioxidant extract. These help preserve your products and add to their skin benefits. Always store your skincare creations in a cool, dark place to maintain their potency and prevent spoilage. Regularly check your products for any changes in smell, color, or texture, which could indicate contamination.

Crafting your own toners and mists allows you to gain control over what goes on your skin and provides it with the specific nourishment it needs. Whether it's the restoring power of a well-balanced toner or the refreshing touch of a hydrating mist, these skincare staples are essential for maintaining healthy, radiant skin. As you experiment with different formulations and discover the best combinations, these products will become indispensable parts of your skincare regime.

The Complete Ritual: Building a Holistic Skincare Routine

Integrating a collection of homemade skincare products into your daily regimen requires thoughtful planning and understanding of how each component—face masks, scrubs, balms, toners, and mists—can be orchestrated to harmonize and enhance your skin's health. To start, visualize your skincare routine as a symphony, where each product plays a specific role, contributing to the overall performance, which, in this case, is your skin's well-being. The key is in selecting the right products and applying them in an order that maximizes their benefits.

Consider setting a foundation with a gentle scrub, ideally used in the morning, to slough off dead cells and rejuvenate your skin, preparing it for the next steps. After cleansing, applying a toner can help restore the pH balance of your skin, refining pores and preparing the skin to absorb the nutrients more effectively from the following treatments. With your skin now primed, a hydrating balm would be your next step, especially if your skin tends towards dryness, as it seals in moisture and provides a barrier against environmental pollutants. Keep a facial mist handy throughout the day to refresh your skin, ensuring it remains hydrated and vibrant. Applying a nourishing face mask in the evening can help address specific skin concerns, such as dryness or oiliness, depending on the ingredients used. This routine covers all bases and ensures that each product is used at an optimal time for the best results.

Creating distinct morning and evening routines is crucial because your skin behaves differently throughout the day. Your skin is protected in the morning, gearing up to shield itself against environmental aggressors like pollution, UV rays, and bacteria. Therefore, your morning routine should focus on protection and fortification. Products with antioxidants, SPF, and light moisturizers fit well into this category. In contrast, the evening is when your skin switches to recovery mode. This is the time for intensive hydrating, repairing, and rejuvenating, as your skin's permeability is higher at night. Hence, products like deep moisturizers, serums rich in active ingredients, and restorative face masks are more effective when used in your nighttime routine.

Adjusting these routines to cater to specific skin concerns such as acne, signs of aging, or persistent dryness involves a dynamic approach. If dealing with acne, consider incorporating products with salicylic acid or tea tree oil, known for their blemish-fighting properties, into your evening routine, when your skin's enhanced absorption abilities can maximize its efficacy. For signs of aging, ingredients like retinol or peptides can be incorporated into night serums or creams, as they help stimulate collagen production and cell turnover. Those with dry skin should focus on layering hydrating products and using more decadent balms or creams in the evening to ensure the skin remains hydrated throughout the night.

Encouraging you to maintain a skincare diary offers a structured way to track your skin's response to various products and routines. This practice helps identify which products work best and understand how changes in your environment, diet, or stress levels affect your skin. Note changes in your skin's texture, new breakouts, or improvements. Over time, this diary will become a valuable resource, guiding you in making informed adjustments to your skincare routine, such as swapping out certain products seasonally or adjusting the frequency of use depending on your skin's condition. This ongoing process of observation and adjustment ensures that your skincare routine remains aligned with your skin's evolving needs, providing optimal care at every stage.

Holistic Skincare for Teens: Safe and Simple Solutions

Navigating the teenage years brings about many changes, not least those affecting the skin. This period of life marks a crucial time for establishing skincare routines that address immediate concerns and set the foundation for future skin health. For teenagers, whose skins are often subjected to hormonal changes that can drive issues like acne, oiliness, and sensitivity, adopting a gentle and effective skincare approach is paramount. This ensures that the skin is cared for without exacerbating existing conditions.

Initiating teens into the basics of skincare involves teaching them the importance of cleansing, moisturizing, and applying sunscreen—three simple steps constituting the cornerstone of any good skincare routine. Cleansing is vital as it helps remove dirt, oil, and impurities that can clog pores and lead to breakouts. However, it's crucial to use gentle cleansers that do not strip the skin of its natural oils, which can trigger an overproduction of oil. Moisturizing helps to maintain the skin's natural barrier, preventing issues caused by dryness and irritation. Even oily skin needs moisturizer; oil-free, non-comedogenic formulas can help maintain balance. Lastly, sunscreen is indispensable in protecting the skin from harmful UV rays, which cause sunburn and contribute to premature aging and skin cancer risks.

Acne is a prevalent issue during adolescence, and managing it naturally can be both practical and reassuring for teens worried about their skin appearance. Ingredients like tea tree oil have natural antibacterial properties that can help manage acne without the harshness of chemical treatments. Similarly, green tea extract can create soothing topical applications that reduce inflammation and redness associated with breakouts. Encouraging homemade masks with natural anti-inflammatory ingredients like oatmeal or aloe vera can also relieve skin repair.

Promoting consistent skincare habits is crucial. Encouraging teens to stick to their skincare routines daily helps to instill habits that can lead to long-term benefits. It's also essential to teach patience; skin transformations will not occur overnight, and over-treating the skin can lead to irritation and other issues. Emphasizing gentle care and consistency over quick fixes encourages teens to take a more measured and practical approach to skincare.

Engaging teens with DIY skincare projects not only makes the process of learning about skincare more enjoyable but also empowers them to take control of their skin health. Simple projects like creating natural lip balms from coconut oil and beeswax or making facial masks from kitchen ingredients like bananas and honey can be fun and educational. These projects teach teens about the properties of natural ingredients and how they can be used to treat different skin conditions. Moreover, it fosters a deeper understanding and appreciation of natural, holistic skincare practices.

By guiding teens through the basics of skincare, addressing common skin concerns with natural solutions, encouraging healthy habits, and involving them in DIY skincare projects, you help them cultivate a skincare routine that is not only effective and safe but also attuned to the principles of holistic health. This approach does more than just solve skin issues— it builds confidence and teaches the value of self-care through natural means, setting a foundation that can benefit them throughout their lives. As this chapter melds into the next, the focus shifts from the specific needs of teenage skin to exploring the vast world of herbal skincare enhancements that can benefit all ages, deepening our connection to the natural world and its benefits.

Chapter 8: The Holistic Skincare Routine

Imagine greeting the morning with a yawn and a vibrant ritual that awakens both your skin and spirit, setting a tone of nourishment and care that carries you through the day. Your skin, a faithful reflection of your inner health and the care you can afford, deserves a morning routine that revitalizes and protects it from the environmental challenges it will face. This chapter is dedicated to crafting a morning skincare ritual that harmonizes with your body's natural rhythms, enhancing your skin's natural glow while shielding it from the daily exposures of modern life.

Morning Glow: Awakening Your Skin Naturally

Gentle Cleansing

Start each day by liberating your skin from the nocturnal renewal process; overnight, your skin works diligently to repair and regenerate. Gentle cleansing is crucial at dawn—it removes any residual products and frees the pores of oils that have surfaced overnight without stripping the skin of its natural moisture. Opt for a cleanser that respects your skin's pH and is free from harsh sulfates. Ingredients like aloe vera and chamomile cleanse and soothe your skin, preparing it for the next steps in your routine. This act of cleansing is not just about purity but about preparing a fresh canvas for the following nourishing ingredients.

Hydration and Protection

After cleansing, it's vital to rehydrate and form a protective barrier against environmental stressors like UV rays and pollution. A natural, hydrating moisturizer that sinks deeply into the skin's layers can be transformative, mainly when it contains ingredients like hyaluronic acid or glycerin, which lock in moisture. Following this, always appreciate the power of good sunscreen. Choose a mineral-based sunscreen that provides a physical barrier against UV rays. This duo of hydration and protection is crucial. At the same time, the moisturizer maintains your skin's hydration levels, and the sunscreen wards off potential damage from the sun, preventing premature aging and promoting long-term skin health.

Energizing Exercises

Incorporate facial exercises or yoga early in your routine to stimulate circulation and oxygen flow to the face. Simple techniques such as gentle tapping or circular motions on the cheeks can invigorate the skin, enhancing your natural glow. Like the downward dog, yoga poses that invert the head can further boost circulation, bringing a rosy, healthy color to your face. This practice not only wakes up your skin but also aligns your energy for the day ahead, making it a form of self-care that beautifies your skin and mood.

Nutritious Breakfast for Skin Health

What you put into your body is just as crucial as what you put on your skin. A breakfast rich in antioxidants and healthy fats can provide the internal nourishment your skin craves. Foods like berries, avocados, and nuts are packed with vitamins and omega-3 fatty acids, which combat inflammation and nourish your skin from the inside out. Consider a smoothie that combines these elements with a splash of almond milk or a bowl of oatmeal topped with fresh fruits and a drizzle of honey. This meal is a delight to consume and a bounty of benefits for your skin, ensuring it receives all it needs to face the day radiantly.

Visual Element: Morning Skincare Infographic An infographic briefly outlines each step to help you visualize and implement this energizing morning routine. From the ideal ingredients in your gentle cleanser to the best yoga poses for boosting facial circulation, this visual guide ensures a quick, handy reference that supports your journey to radiant morning skin.

By dedicating time each morning to nurture your skin, you enhance its health and appearance and set a positive, caring tone for the day ahead. This morning ritual is an act of love, a way to connect with yourself and prepare for the day's challenges with resilience and radiance. As you blend these practices into your daily life, they become more than just steps in skincare— they evolve into a joyful celebration of self-care and awareness, highlighting the profound connection between how we care for ourselves and how we show up in the world.

Nighttime Nourishment: Restorative Practices for Evening

As the day winds down, your skin deserves a moment to breathe and rejuvenate just as much as you do. The evening presents an ideal time to focus on deep cleaning and nourishing your skin, allowing you to address the accumulation of pollutants and makeup that can clog pores and accelerate aging. An oil-based cleanser is your first step in this nighttime ritual. Unlike traditional cleansers that might strip the skin of natural oils, oil-based cleansers dissolve stubborn makeup and debris gently yet effectively. This method, known as double cleansing, starts with an oil cleanser followed by a water-based cleanser. The oil interacts with your skin's natural lipids and removes grease-based impurities such as sebum, SPF, and pollutants. Following up with a water-based cleanser removes any remaining impurities and water-based debris, leaving your skin pristine and ready to absorb the beneficial ingredients of overnight treatments.

Overnight treatments are akin to a silent therapist for your skin, working diligently to repair, rejuvenate, and hydrate as you sleep. These treatments come in various forms, such as night-specific serums, hydrating masks, or even spot treatments, and they often contain active ingredients that are too potent for daytime use under sunlight. Ingredients such as retinoids and peptides in serums can accelerate cell turnover, boost collagen production, fight fine lines, and improve skin texture. Hydrating masks might contain higher concentrations of hyaluronic acid, which deeply moisturizes and plumps the skin overnight, ensuring you wake up with a dewy complexion. Applying these treatments is not just a task—it's a ritual that prepares your skin for a night of healing and regeneration.

Pre-sleep activities can significantly influence your sleep quality and your skin's health. Incorporating relaxation techniques into your evening routine can profoundly impact your stress levels and, consequently, your skin's appearance. Consider setting aside time to unwind with a book or a brief meditation session. This mental downshift helps decrease cortisol levels, a stress hormone that can exacerbate skin issues like acne and eczema. Meditation, even for a few minutes, can also enhance your overall sleep quality, providing your skin ample time to undergo its natural repair processes. This intentional quieting of the mind prepares your body for rest and sets a serene foundation for your skin to rejuvenate.

Creating a sleep-friendly environment plays a crucial role in this nocturnal skin therapy. Your bedroom should be a sanctuary that promotes deep, uninterrupted sleep. Consider optimizing your sleeping area by ensuring your room is dark, quiet, and calm. Blackout curtains, eye masks, or low-wavelength light bulbs can help regulate your sleep cycles better, while white noise machines or earplugs can minimize noise disruptions. The temperature of your room also affects sleep quality; more relaxed environments generally enhance sleep, which is crucial for cellular repair and regeneration. Each element of your sleep environment should support a restful night, directly contributing to your skin's ability to heal and rejuvenate. By fostering these conditions, you enhance your sleep quality and ensure that your skin receives the maximum benefit from your nighttime skincare practices, making each morning a revelation of refreshed, vibrant skin.

The Weekly Pamper: Planning Your Skincare Rituals

A weekly pampering session allows you to show extra love and care for your skin, addressing needs that daily routines might overlook. This dedicated time allows for more profound interventions to reset and rejuvenate your skin's health, keeping it vibrant and resilient. Let's explore some essential weekly practices that can transform how your skin looks and feels, focusing on exfoliation, deep hydration, self-massage, and detoxifying treatments designed to enhance your skin's natural beauty and clarity.

Exfoliation

Exfoliation is a critical component of any comprehensive skincare routine. It involves the removal of dead skin cells that accumulate on the surface, which can lead to dullness, flakiness, and clogged pores. Natural ingredients can be your best allies for a gentle yet effective exfoliation. Consider using a soft, finely ground almond meal, which, when mixed with a soothing agent like oat milk, forms a paste that can gently lift away dead skin cells without the harshness often associated with synthetic exfoliants.

Apply this mixture in slow, circular motions over your face to promote blood flow while the granules do their work. Another excellent choice is rice bran, rich in vitamins and minerals and known for its skin-brightening properties. When mixed with a touch of honey, it not only exfoliates but also imparts a natural glow to your complexion. Consistency and gentleness are essential to successful exfoliation; doing it once a week is usually sufficient to keep your skin fresh and ready to absorb other products more effectively.

Deep Hydration Session

Hydration is paramount for maintaining skin elasticity and preventing premature aging. However, during the dryer months, your skin may require more intensive hydration than your regular moisturizer can provide. This is where layering hydration products come into play. Start with a lightweight serum that contains hyaluronic acid, which draws moisture into the skin. Follow this with a gel-based moisturizer that adds another layer of hydration, and seal it all in with a heavier cream or overnight mask that locks in moisture. This technique ensures that the skin receives moisture from multiple sources and at different depths, which helps combat the drying effects of harsh climates. Additionally, consider using a humidifier in your room during the night. It adds moisture to the air, which can help prevent your skin from drying out and keep it plump and radiant.

Self-Massage Techniques

Facial massages can transform your skincare routine into a therapeutic ritual, enhancing product absorption and promoting circulation while relieving muscle tension in the face. Start with clean hands and a few drops of facial oil that suit your skin type. Begin at the chin and use gentle upward strokes along your jawline to the ears. Use circular motions around your cheekbones to relieve tension and enhance blood flow. Remember the forehead; smooth from the center towards the temples. This routine helps your skin absorb products better and eases the day's stress, smoothing out the fine lines that can form from facial expressions. Performing this massage weekly can lead to visible improvements in skin tone and firmness over time.

Detoxifying Practices

Detoxifying your skin is crucial for maintaining clarity and preventing breakouts. Clay masks are particularly effective for drawing out impurities from the pores. Bentonite clay, for instance, has a strong negative electric charge when hydrated, which helps it pull out positively charged toxins. Mix the clay with apple cider vinegar, which helps to balance your skin's pH, and apply the mask once a week for a deep cleanse. Leave it on for 10 to 15 minutes—just enough time for the clay to dry, but not so long that it causes skin dehydration. Rinsing off with lukewarm water can reveal refreshed, smooth, and detoxified skin, making this practice a potent addition to your weekly skincare rituals.

Incorporating these practices into your weekly skincare routine provides a structured yet flexible regimen that caters to deeper skin needs, promoting renewal and maintenance that daily routines might miss. Each of these steps brings you closer to achieving a skin condition that is healthy and resilient against the stresses of daily life and environmental exposure. Whether through gentle exfoliation, layered hydration, therapeutic massage, or effective detoxification, your commitment to this weekly pampering session will reflect in your skin's enduring beauty and vitality.

Stress Less: Mindfulness and Meditation for Skin Health

The skin, often called the body's largest organ, is also one of the most sensitive barometers for internal stress. It's no secret that periods of high stress can manifest externally, exacerbating conditions like acne, eczema, and psoriasis. This is primarily due to the body's stress response, including cortisol release.

This hormone can increase oil production in your skin's sebaceous glands, leading to acne, and can also inflame and aggravate other skin conditions. To combat these effects, incorporating mindfulness and meditation into your daily routine can be a game-changer, offering a dual benefit for both mental calm and skin clarity.

Introducing mindfulness into your daily life doesn't have to be a daunting task. It can be as simple as practicing mindful breathing for a few minutes daily. This involves focusing entirely on your breath, feeling the air in and out of your lungs, and observing the sensations throughout your body. This practice helps center your thoughts and lowers stress levels, reducing the likelihood of stress-related skin flare-ups. Another effective mindfulness exercise involves mindful observation, which can be done anywhere at any time. This might include observing a leaf's details, the fabric's texture, or the components of a complex scent. Focusing intently on these details shifts your mind away from stressors and toward active engagement in the present moment, promoting peace and calm.

For those new to meditation, the practice may seem intimidating, but it's pretty accessible and can be profoundly beneficial for both mental and skin health. Start with guided meditations, available through various apps and online platforms. These guides provide step-by-step instructions and can help you navigate the process of calming the mind. Initially, you should aim for short sessions, five to ten minutes each, gradually increasing the duration as you become more comfortable with the practice. The key is consistency; even a few minutes of meditation each day can reduce overall stress levels, improving your skin's health and appearance over time.

Creating a calming evening skincare routine incorporating these practices can further enhance your skin's ability to repair and rejuvenate overnight. Consider setting aside extra time in the evening to perform your skincare regimen as a meditative ritual. Apply each product slowly and with intention, using the time to focus intensely on the sensations you experience— the texture of the skincare products, the scent, the feeling of your fingers on your skin. This not only enhances the effectiveness of the products by encouraging thorough application and improving circulation through gentle massage but also turns your skincare routine into a relaxing, stress-reducing ritual that soothes your mind and prepares you for a restful night's sleep. Embracing these mindfulness and meditation practices as integral parts of your skincare routine helps forge a more robust mental and skin health connection. By reducing stress through these mindful practices, you enhance your skin's appearance and improve your overall well-being. As you continue to explore these techniques, you'll likely discover a more peaceful mind and a more transparent, more radiant complexion, reflecting the profound impact of internal wellness on external beauty.

As this chapter concludes, remember that the health of your skin is deeply tied to the peace of your mind. The practices outlined here are designed to nurture both, guiding you toward a state of calm that radiates from the inside out. The next chapter will build upon these foundational techniques, introducing advanced strategies to enhance your holistic skincare journey further. Embrace these practices, and watch as they transform your skin and your entire personal wellness approach.

Chapter 9: Community and Connection

Imagine standing in a lush garden, where every plant thrives on the care of the gardener and through the symbiotic relationships with its surrounding flora. Similarly, the journey of holistic skincare blossoms fully when nurtured within a community. Whether it's sharing insights, exchanging tips, or simply offering encouragement, a skincare circle's collective wisdom and support can be transformative. This chapter delves into the heart of forming and flourishing within these supportive communities, enhancing our skincare practices and enriching our social well-being.

Skincare Circles: Forming Supportive Communities

The Benefits of Skincare Circles

Skincare circles, at their core, are groups of individuals who share a common interest in enhancing their knowledge and practices around skincare. Joining or forming such circles offers a plethora of benefits. Firstly, shared learning in a community setting can significantly accelerate your understanding and appreciation of skincare. Each member brings unique experiences and insights, contributing to a rich reservoir of knowledge from which all members can draw. Secondly, these circles provide encouragement and motivation. It's easier to stick to a skincare regimen or try new treatments when you are part of a group that cheers each other on. Lastly, inherent accountability comes with regular meetings and discussions. It helps maintain consistency in your skincare routines, which is crucial for seeing long-term results.

Starting a Skincare Circle

Begin by identifying what you hope to achieve through this skincare circle. Is it to explore natural skincare remedies, to share experiences with commercial products, or to learn more about dermatological science? Clear goals will help attract like-minded individuals who share your aspirations. Finding members can be as simple as starting conversations in online forums, local community boards, or even within your circle of friends and family. Once you have a few interested members, organize an initial meeting to discuss everyone's goals and expectations. It's also helpful to establish a regular schedule for online or in-person meetings to maintain the group's momentum. As the circle grows, roles such as coordinator or communicator can be assigned to help manage the group dynamics and logistics.

Online Communities and Forums

In today's digital age, online platforms are vital for connecting people with similar interests. They offer a broader reach and the convenience of accessing collective knowledge from the comfort of your home. Websites like

Reddit, skincare-specific forums, and social media groups are goldmines for such interactions. They allow for sharing a wide range of topics, from personal skincare routines to the latest scientific research in dermatology. Engaging in these platforms can also help promote your local skincare circle, attract new members, and even organize virtual meet-ups that include discussions, guest speakers, and more.

Skincare Circle Activities

Consider various activities to keep the circle engaging and beneficial for all members. Group DIY skincare sessions can be fun and interactive to learn about and experiment with new recipes. Each member could bring a different natural ingredient, sharing its benefits and uses, followed by a session of making facemasks or scrubs together. Product swaps are another exciting activity, where members bring skincare products that didn't work for them but might benefit someone else. This helps you recycle products and discover new ones that could suit your skin better. Additionally, inviting a dermatologist or skincare expert as a guest speaker can provide professional insights and answer members' questions. These activities enhance learning and strengthen the community's bonds, making each meeting something to look forward to.

Fostering these skincare circles enhances your own skincare journey and contributes to a community that values health, beauty, and connection. Each circle becomes a microcosm of shared growth and support, echoing the broader movement towards holistic wellness and sustainable beauty practices. As you engage and contribute to these communities, remember that every tip shared, every product recommended, and every success celebrated adds a leaf to this ever-growing garden of collective skincare wisdom.

Sharing the Glow: Skincare as a Bonding Activity

Traditionally viewed as a personal regimen, skincare holds untapped potential as a medium for bonding and nurturing relationships with friends and family. Integrating skincare into your social interactions enriches these connections and transforms routine practices into shared, joyful experiences. Envision a casual Sunday at home, where you invite a friend over for a skincare session instead of the usual solitary routine. You explore various facemasks together, discuss your skincare favorites, and share tips that have transformed your routines. This shared experience does more than beautify the skin—it creates a space for laughter, conversation, and connection, deepening bonds in a relaxed, nurturing environment.

Planning skincare-themed parties or gatherings can take this concept to a larger group, making it an ideal activity for birthdays, bridal showers, or a much-needed girls' night. Set up mask-making stations using natural ingredients like oats, honey, and yogurt, where guests can customize their masks. Add a mini-facial station equipped with gentle cleansers, moisturizers, and various serums to suit different skin types. Provide soft towels, headbands, and mirrors to complete the experience. As the host, prepare a brief demonstration or share a presentation on the benefits of each ingredient, turning the event into an informative and fun learning experience. These gatherings provide a unique way to celebrate and encourage a hands-on approach to skincare, promoting self-care among your guests.

Extending the glow to younger generations involves mindful education about natural skincare and early establishing healthy routines. Consider the impact of setting aside time to teach your children, nieces, nephews, or younger siblings about caring for their skin with natural ingredients. Simple activities like making an essential honey mask or a cucumber toner can be fascinating and fun for children, providing them with knowledge that promotes long-term wellness. Explain the role of each ingredient and its benefits to the skin, fostering a sense of curiosity and respect for natural skincare practices. This educates them on how to care for their skin and instills values of sustainability and health from a young age.

The concept of community service through skincare opens yet another avenue for extending care beyond personal benefits to societal contributions. Volunteering at organizations that support individuals with skin conditions can provide emotional and practical support to those in need. Organize or participate in workshops that teach natural skincare routines to people undergoing medical treatments that affect their skin, offering methods to gently soothe and nourish their skin. Consider starting a project that collects unused or gently used skincare products to donate to shelters, helping those in less fortunate circumstances to access quality skincare. These acts of service not only aid those in need but also enrich your experience, highlighting the profound impact that sharing knowledge and resources can have on community well-being in a profound and meaningful way.

Skincare transcends its traditional role through these activities, becoming a bridge that connects generations, enhances friendships, and supports communities. It evolves into a shared journey of discovery, health, and wellness, emphasizing the importance of taking care of oneself and those around us. Integrating these practices into your life will illuminate paths to better skin-enriched relationships and a strengthened com-munity.

The Gift of Beauty: DIY Skincare Gifts

Giving speaks volumes, especially when the gifts are infused with personal touches and thoughtful consideration. Imagine the delight and appreciation of receiving a handmade skincare gift tailored to your specific skin needs and preferences. This intelligent gift-giving approach enhances the connection between the giver and the receiver and introduces them to the enriching world of natural skincare. Crafting personalized skincare gifts, whether for birthdays, holidays, or special occasions, allows you to express your care and creativity, making each gift a unique expression of appreciation and affection.

Creating personalized skincare gifts begins with understand-ing the recipient's skin type and any specific skin concerns they might have. This thoughtful consideration ensures that each product in the gift set not only delights but also benefits the recipient. For instance, if your friend has dry skin, a homemade rich moisturizing cream or a hydrating serum can make a thoughtful gift. For those with a more oily complexion, a natural clay mask or a light, non-comedogenic facial oil might be more suitable. Adding a personal touch, such as infusing the cream with their favorite scent or including a handwritten note explaining the benefits of each item, can make the gift even more special and heartfelt.

Packaging and presentation are pivotal in transforming your homemade skincare products into enchanting gifts. Consider sustainable and aesthetically pleasing materials that enhance the overall appeal and reflect the natural ethos of the products. Glass jars, metal tins, and bamboo containers look elegant and eco-friendly. You can decorate these containers with natural twine, recycled paper labels, and even dried flowers to add a personal and charming touch. For wrapping, use biodegradable paper or a beautiful reusable cloth, embracing the art of furoshiki, the Japanese fabric wrapping technique. Each packaging element can be thoughtfully selected to complement the gift's theme and the recipient's style, making the unboxing experience delightful and memorable.

For those special occasions that call for something extra, curating themed skincare gift sets can add an element of excitement and exclusivity. During the holiday season, a winter care package featuring a rich hand cream, a moisturizing lip balm, and a hydrating facial serum can be perfect for combating the harsh winter air. Alternatively, for a relaxation-themed gift, include items like a lavender-infused facial mist, a soothing herbal face mask, and a silky eye pillow. Each themed set caters to the specific needs brought about by the season or occasion and provides a complete and immersive experience for the recipient.

Including recipes and instructions with your skincare gifts is a thoughtful way to engage the recipient further with DIY skincare. This inclusion adds value to the gift and empowers the recipient to recreate their favorite products or even explore their formulations. A beautifully designed booklet or a set of elegant cards detailing each product's purpose, ingredients, and steps for creation can serve as a practical and educational addition to your gift. This gesture enhances the personal touch and encourages a deeper appreciation and understanding of natural skincare, potentially inspiring the recipient to embrace and explore holistic skincare practices on their own.

DIY skincare gifts offer a unique opportunity to convey affection and consideration in a tangible form through the careful selection of ingredients, thoughtful packaging, and the inclusion of personalized elements. Each gift set becomes a testament to the thought, care, and creativity invested in its creation, making it much more than just a present—it becomes a meaningful connection, a sharing of wellness and beauty personalized to the recipient's unique tastes and needs. As you craft these gifts, each choice—from the ingredients to the packaging—reflects your personal touch and deep regard for the recipient, ensuring that each gift is received with joy and cherished as a symbol of thoughtfulness and care.

Spreading the Word: Educating Others on Holistic Practices

In the vibrant landscape of holistic skincare, the beauty of your knowledge is magnified when shared with others. It's like planting a seed that sprouts into a flourishing garden of awareness and empowerment. Every conversation, whether online or in the heart of your community, can sow the seeds for a transformative approach to beauty. You are armed with invaluable insights into the benefits of natural, non-toxic skincare, and each time you share these insights, you advocate for healthier choices and contribute to a more significant cultural shift towards sustainable beauty practices.

Encouraging you to take your passion for holistic skincare beyond personal practice, consider the impactful role you can play in educating others. Organizing workshops and talks provides a structured platform for sharing your knowledge. Start by identifying key topics that resonate most with your audience: the basics of creating a skincare routine, the benefits of specific natural ingredients, or ways to decipher product labels. Venues such as community centers, local libraries, or even online platforms can be ideal settings for these events. Engaging activities, such as live demonstrations or interactive Q&A sessions, can enhance the learning experience, making the information more accessible and applicable. Furthermore, consider partnering with local wellness centers or eco-friendly businesses to broaden your reach. This draws on a broader audience and supports local enterprises that share your commitment to sustainable practices.

In today's digital age, writing and blogging offer potent tools for spreading your message to a global audience. Starting a blog dedicated to holistic skincare can attract readers seeking guidance and inspiration on transitioning to natural beauty routines. Share your experiences, product reviews, and tips for naturally maintaining skin health. To increase your blog's visibility, engage with other bloggers or influencers who share similar values, contributing guest posts or collaborating on content. This extended online presence can significantly amplify your impact, helping to inform and inspire a broader audience about the benefits of clean, continental skincare.

Advocacy is crucial in the movement towards cleaner, safer beauty products. By staying informed about the regulations and standards governing skincare products, you can help push for higher transparency and safety in the beauty industry. Support organizations and initiatives that lobby for stricter ingredient scrutiny and labeling laws. Use your platforms, be they social gatherings, workshops, or online blogs, to educate others about the importance of these issues. Encourage them to support legislative changes that protect consumers from harmful chemicals commonly found in beauty products.

Each voice added to this cause can drive significant change, shifting industry standards towards more ethical practices.

By stepping into the role of an educator and advocate, you enrich your understanding and empower others to make informed choices about their skincare. This ripple effect of knowledge and empowerment fosters a community that values health, sustainability, and transparency, contributing to a more continental approach to beauty that resonates well beyond individual practices.

As this chapter closes, we reflect on the powerful impact of community and communication in holistic skincare. From forming supportive circles to sharing knowledge and advocating for cleaner beauty standards, each action you take propels the movement towards a healthier, more sustainable approach to skincare. These community-focused efforts enhance individual lives and forge a collective path toward a more informed and conscious society. As we turn the page, the next chapter will explore advanced natural skincare techniques that build upon these foundational practices, offering deeper insights and more refined strategies for enhancing your holistic skincare journey.

Conclusion

As we conclude our journey together through the "Wholey Face Masks" pages, I hope you feel a sense of empowerment and enlightenment. This book was crafted to guide you away from the chemical-laden landscape of conventional skincare and towards a more natural, nurturing approach. Together, we've explored how everyday ingredients can transform your skin and overall well-being.

From the Dangers to the Delights

We unveiled the harsh realities hidden in commercial skincare products, emphasizing the urgent need for awareness and change. Moving through the chapters, we shifted our focus to the bountiful alternatives provided by nature—avocado, honey, lavender, and more—that promise and deliver beauty and health in their purest forms.

Empowerment Through Knowledge and Action

Each chapter is built upon the last, equipping you with the knowledge to make informed decisions about your skincare.

We explored the practical aspects of creating your face masks, understanding your skin's needs, and adapting your choices to those needs. The recipes and techniques are designed to be adaptable and forgiving, inviting you to experiment and find what works for you.

A Call to Holistic Health

Beyond recipes and ingredients, this book has been an invitation to embrace a holistic approach to beauty. It's about seeing the connection between your skin, body, and the environment. I encourage you to continue exploring, learning, and advocating for skincare that respects human and environmental health.

Next Steps

As you turn the final pages of this book, do not see it as the end but as a beginning. Start by trying a few recipes, perhaps sharing them with friends or family. Pay attention to how your skin responds, and let your experiences guide you to further personalization.

Writing this book has been a journey of discovery and affirmation. Every word and recipe shared with you reflects my commitment to a healthier, more sustainable world. I am immensely grateful for the opportunity to share this part of my life with you, and I hope it inspires you to embrace the beauty of natural skincare.

Thank you for joining me on this beautiful journey. May you continue to find joy and health on your path to holistic beauty. Remember, the most radiant skin reflects a nurtured soul and a respected environment. Here's to your health, inside and out!

Also by LaDonna Naturale

Rediscovering You: A 30 Day Self-care Guide for Modern Living

Begin your transformative journey of self-discovery and well-being with "Rediscovering You," a comprehensive 30-day self-care guide tailored for the demands of modern living. This empowering book is designed to guide you through intentional and introspective practices, helping you reconnect with yourself in the midst of life's hustle.As the foundation of my self-care series, this book, "Rediscovering You: A 30 Day Self-care Guide for Modern Living" explains the importance of self-care and gives you practical ways to exercise self-care daily even in our busy modern-day lives.

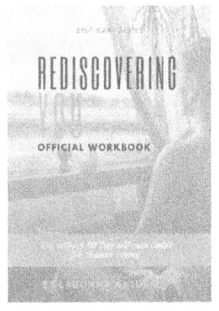

Rediscovering You: Official Self Care Workbook

This Rediscovering You OFFICIAL WORK-BOOK goes along with the book above and includes journal prompts, planning pages, and self-care activities to help you make self-care a habit for the next 30 days.

Cleanse & Reclaim: Detoxify Your Home for a Healthier Life

Unlock a healthier, toxin-free lifestyle in just 30 days, even if you've never embarked on a clean-living journey before.

Introducing a comprehensive, easily digestible guide designed to empower you to reclaim your home from harmful toxins.

With this transformative manual, detoxifying your home can be a stress-free, accessible, budget-friendly, and enjoyable journey!